MY SPIRITUAL
FIRST AID KIT

WORDS OF WISDOM FOR IMMEDIATE RELIEF

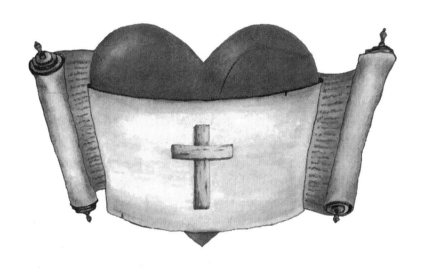

MANNA KO, PHD, HHP, CCN, CCH

ALSO BY MANNA KO

NOTE TO THE READER

While the author and publisher have used their best efforts in preparing and writing this book, they make no representations or warranties with respect to the accuracy or completeness of the contents of this book and specifically disclaim any implied warranties of merchantability, health and/or fitness for a particular purpose. No warranty may be created or extended by sales representatives or written sales materials. The ideas, advice and/or strategies contained herein may not be suitable for your situation, personality, beliefs, health circumstances, and/or lifestyle. Neither the author nor the publisher, or any sponsors of any of this information in the publication shall be responsible for the user's use of any such information. Nothing in this book should be construed as counseling, therapy, legal, medical or other professional advice. The information in this publication should NOT be construed as a claim or representation that any of the information constitutes a specific cure or is palliative. The information should be considered as entertainment or informational only, and is not accepted as conventional procedure(s) deemed necessary and appropriate by the user's attending licensed doctor and/or health care provider.

To my faithful teacher, loyal companion, unwavering confidante, and best friend:

Because of You, I am free and a slave to no one.

You alone have given me more than I dared to ask for, more than I deserve, and more than I can dream of. Your belief in me, love for me, and the sacrifices You've made for me, keep me in awe daily.

I am in constant wonder of you and Your matchless love. You are my inspiration, my joy, my heart, and my life.

I am nothing without You, and want nothing but You.

Thank you, Jesus, for the gift of life… and for the gift of Your life to save my own.

TABLE OF CONTENTS

Foreword   **1**

Introduction   **3**

Are You Tired?   **7**

My Spiritual First-Aid Remedies For:

Anxiousness: When I am uncertain or troubled   9

Belonging: When I feel alone or separated   13

Courage: When I am intimidated or fearful and need to be bold   17

Deliverance: When my enemies or the bondage of negative thoughts and lifestyles torment me   21

Direction: When I am feeling lost and need God's guidance   27

Discernment: When I need clarity in my situation to make healthier choices   33

Discipleship: When I need instruction to live a fruitful life   37

Encouragement: When I am disappointed or disheartened and none of my efforts seem to make a difference   41

Faith: When I question myself, or God, in the midst of my difficulties — 46

Favor: When I need breakthrough and heaven's help for a specific goal, focus, or season in life — 53

Forgiveness: When I feel ashamed of my mistakes or when my heart needs softening — 57

Friendship: To know Who my BEST FRIEND truly is and to build relationships based on His example — 62

Generosity: When I need to think of others more than myself — 70

Grace: When I need a second chance through God's amazing love for me — 75

Gratitude: To be thankful for all my blessings regardless of the circumstances — 79

Healing: When I need the tender touch of God, the Great Physician, for my heart, mind, soul, spirit, and body — 82

Hope: When I feel desperate or lost, and need to remember God's promises and timing are perfect — 88

Humility (Humbleness): To be freed from the shackles of my insecurities and pride (ego) — 95

Inspiration: When I feel unmotivated, insecure, or when I encounter ongoing obstacles — 104

Joy: To celebrate and praise God for my life and all He's done for me — 109

Knowledge and Understanding: When I need God's wisdom and revelation for my situation — 113

Love: To experience God's love, and then to share it with others — 126

Mercy: When I need to be kinder, more compassionate, and less judgmental — 132

Nurturing: When I'm in need of God's tender arms of comfort — 137

Obedience: When I am tempted into wrongdoing or insist on my own way — 141

Peace: When I need assurance in the midst of uncertainties — 151

Perseverance: When I am stretched, overwhelmed, and feel like giving up — 156

Purpose: To know that God has uniquely created me for a special calling — 161

Quietness: When I need uninterrupted time with God to hear His voice — 168

Rest: When I am weary — 174

Restoration: For God to renew me, and to return all the things the enemy has stolen from me — 178

Salvation: To rejoice knowing that I am saved and will live with God forever — 186

Strength: When I am weak and need God's power over my situation   193

Success: To know what my true wealth and accomplishments are   198

Truth: To know the truth in each of life's situations through the unfailing timelessness of God's Word   205

Unity: When the enemy has caused division and dissention within my family, friendships, or community   219

Victory: Because Jesus is my provider and protector, I am victorious in any situation   223

Worship: To praise God for Who He is and for all He has done   231

"X": For any variable that life throws at me   237

Yielding: To surrender and trust in God's better plan for me instead   243

Zealousness: To glorify God by living a purposeful life as I joyfully contribute to others   247

Dear Friend   253

An Invitation   257

FOREWORD

A veteran pubic speaker, counselor, and business advisor with clients in over eight countries, Manna takes her education, skills, gifts, and experience to the very edge in all that she does.

As an enormously talented trainer and Life and Business Strategist, she helps others successfully run their race, boldly cross the finish line, and dive into their destinies.

Manna now brings us this spot-on, quick-reference tool that keeps up with our high-speed culture, and stands as a clear vanguard of the immediate and eternal reliability of God's Word to face life issues.

Gary Goodell
Author and Mentor with Third Day Churches

INTRODUCTION

Life has a relative measure of predictability and certainty to it. The sun rises and sets daily. Dogs like to go for walks and chase tennis balls, and for most of us, alarm clocks wake us up on weekday mornings launching us into a series of more predictable situations. There is also a lot of unpredictability in our lives.

Unpredictable situations often awaken us to the possibilities of having more, being more, and living more than the simple or even numbing habits and routines we've manufactured, and even settled for. But first, we have to overcome the disappointment – and even shock of these unexpected circumstances. What do we do when the unpredictable occurs? How do we face sudden chaos in our lives?

In this book, you will find something that makes sense of the chaos, something that takes the broken pieces in your life and makes them whole. Yes, there is something that can bring stability to the shaky areas of your life, something which will bless you beyond imagination and beyond measure—through good times and bad, for richer or poorer, in sickness and in health.

That "something" is actually "Someone," and this "Someone" will never forsake you, no matter what you may have done, no matter what has been done to you, and no matter what is happening in your life.

You see, the world's definition of peace is the "absence" of something – conflict, disagreements, wars, etc. But for those who believe in Jesus Christ, peace is the "presence" of Someone – of

Jesus, Who shelters us and provides for us no matter what is happening around us.

Furthermore, the world's definitions of love, success, power, and "living the good life" are often dependent on the moods and whims of other people, or the next new "thing". Our society is overwhelmed with fads, trends, and the fickleness of desires that are borne out of the dissatisfaction and lack of clarity in our hearts. Hence, the world's definition of love, success, power, and "living the good life" is often superficial, temporary, unstable. Sadly, more often than not, it fosters envy, jealousy, division and distance in relationships.

We are never satisfied with ourselves because we are never satisfied *within* ourselves.

The motivational "1-2-3" and "how-to" books, tools, workshops, etc. may be useful, but as good as they are for some moderate behavioral or mindset changes, they are temporary at best, and manipulative at worst. Please don't misunderstand me. Some of these ideas and tools may be very helpful, but not one of these programs can fully address the deep and mysterious longings in our lives. Not one of these programs fully meets the cry of our wounded hearts or our hungry and searching souls (even though many claim to). I can say this because I have spent decades, and thousands of dollars, taking dozens of these programs, trying to find answers and remedies for the confusing situations in my own life. And I know hundreds of people who have done the same thing, all without achieving success.

Although these courses offered good ideas and tools, they mostly only masked or managed the hurts. They never addressed the core issues, and they certainly did not provide effective options or solutions that brought about transformation.

However, when I went back to the Truth, and allowed the Holy Spirit to minister to me, I was not only comforted and encouraged— insights, revelation of strategies, wisdom and answers were downloaded to me. So, yes, after trying many other approaches, and after personally working with hundreds of people and organizations, I can truly say, only God's Word can simultaneously meet the deepest, and the highest of our spiritual needs.

Helen Keller once said, "The only thing worse than being blind is having sight but no vision." In order for transformation to occur, it's critical for us to see things differently.

When we allow ourselves to have a new and higher vision for our lives—to see life from God's perspective—we free ourselves from old patterns that no longer have valid applications and liberate ourselves to choose more life-generating responses. We don't have to be prisoners or captives without hope.

Are you open to living an empowered life? Are you open to living a life of courage, vision and purpose, no matter what unexpected situations arise? Are you open to breaking the old default patterns that cause stagnancy, frustration, bitterness, and yet another journey around the same mountain? Are you open to receiving Words of Truth to "overcome", instead of being "overrun", by the circumstances of life? Are you willing to be greater than mere circumstances?

If you said "yes" to the above questions, then you are in the right place!

All things are possible!

There is a timeless, secure, and trustworthy Source that you can really count on, and no market conditions, environmental conditions, or emotional temperaments will ever shake it!

Your disappointments and discouragements can be turned back into fulfilled dreams. Your brokenness can be healed, and the defeats you've experienced can be restored and redeemed so you can live purposefully, abundantly, joyfully, victoriously, and triumphantly!

Allow this book to be a beginning step for you. See it as a GPS or road map that gives you direction if you've lost your way.

It's all at your fingertips…simply turn the page and start living the extraordinarily magnificent life you were meant to experience, no matter what the circumstances may be!

In joyful, loving service,

Manna Ko

San Diego, California, 2014

ARE YOU TIRED?

Are you tired?

Worn out? Burned out on religion?

Come to Me.

Get away with Me, and you'll recover your life.

I'll show you how to take a real rest.

Walk with Me and work with Me—watch how I do it.

Learn the unforced rhythms of grace.

I won't lay anything heavy or ill-fitting on you. Keep company with Me, and you'll learn to live freely and lightly.

Love, God

Matthew 11:28-30 THE MESSAGE

ANXIOUSNESS

When I am uncertain or troubled

Be anxious for nothing, but in everything by prayer and supplication, with thanksgiving, let your requests be made known to God; and the peace of God, which surpasses all understanding, will guard your hearts and minds through Christ Jesus.

Philippians 4:6-7 NKJV

'I AM the Alpha and the Omega, the Beginning, and the End', says the Lord, 'Who is, and Who was, and Who is to come, the Almighty.'

Revelation 1:8 NKJV

The LORD your God is with you wherever you go.

Joshua 1:9 NKJV

And this is the confidence that we have in Him, that if we ask anything according to His will, He hears us. And if we know that He hears us, whatever we ask, we know that we have the petitions that we have asked of Him.

1 John 5:14-15 NKJV

Has anyone by fussing before the mirror ever gotten taller by so much as an inch? If fussing can't even do that, why fuss at all? Walk into the fields and look at the wildflowers. They don't fuss with their appearance - but have you ever seen color and design quite like it? The ten best-dressed men and women in the country look shabby alongside them. If God gives such attention to the wildflowers, most of them never even seen, don't you think He'll attend to you, take pride in you, do His best for you? What I'm trying to do here is get you to relax, not be so preoccupied with getting so you can respond to God's giving. People who don't know God and the way He works, fuss over these things, but you know both God and how He works. Steep yourself in God-reality, God-initiative, God-provisions. You'll find all your everyday human concerns will be met. Don't be afraid of missing out. You're my dearest friends! The Father wants to give you the very kingdom itself.

Luke 12:28-30 THE MESSAGE

For God is not the author of confusion, but of peace...

1 Corinthians 13:33 NIV

Dear friend, guard clear thinking and common sense with your life. Don't for a minute lose sight of them. They'll keep your soul alive and well, they'll keep you fit and attractive. You'll travel safely. You'll neither tire nor trip. You'll take afternoon naps without a worry, and you'll enjoy a good night's sleep. No need to panic over alarms or surprises, or predictions that doomsday's just around the corner, because God will be right there with you. He'll keep you safe and sound.

Proverbs 3:21-26 THE MESSAGE

Now may our Lord Jesus Christ Himself, and our God and Father, Who has loved us and give us everlasting consolation and good hope by grace, comfort your hearts and establish you in every good word and work.

2 Thessalonians 2:16-17 NKJV

May the God of hope fill you with all joy and peace as you trust in Him, so that you may overflow with hope by the power of the Holy Spirit.

Romans 15:13 NIV

You will keep him in perfect peace, whose mind is stayed on You, because he trusts in You. Trust in the LORD forever for the LORD is everlasting strength.

Isaiah 26:3-4 NKJV

For the LORD will be your confidence, and will keep your foot from being caught.

Proverbs 3:26 NKJV

But they that wait upon the LORD shall renew their strength; they shall mount up with wings as eagles. They shall run, and not be weary, and they shall walk and not faint.

Isaiah 40:31 NKJV

But as it is written: 'Eye has not seen, nor ear heard, nor have entered into the heart of man the things which God has prepared for those who love Him.'

1 Corinthians 2:9 NKJV

Peace I leave with you. My peace I give to you; not as the world gives, but as I give to you. Let not your heart be troubled, neither let it be afraid.

John 14:27 NKJV

Be strong and of good courage, do not fear nor be afraid of them; for the LORD your God, He is the One who goes with you. He will not leave you nor forsake you.

Deuteronomy 31:6 NKJV

A final word: Be strong in the Lord and in His mighty power. Put on all of God's armor so that you will be able to stand firm against all the strategies of the devil. For we are not fighting against flesh and blood enemies, but against evil rulers and authorities of the unseen world, against mighty powers in this dark world, and against evil spirits in the heavenly places. Therefore, put on every piece of God's armor so you will be able to resist the enemy in the time of evil. Then after the battle, you will be standing firm. Stand your ground, putting on the belt of truth and the body armor of God's righteousness. For shoes, put on the peace that comes from the Good News so that you will be fully prepared. In addition to all of these, hold up the shield of faith to stop the fiery arrows of the devil. Put on salvation as your helmet, and take the sword of the Spirit, which is the Word of God. Pray in the Spirit at all times and on every occasion. Stay alert and be persistent in your prayers for all believers everywhere.

Ephesians 6:10-18 NLT

BELONGING

When I feel alone or separated

*I have even called you by your name. I have named you,
though you have not known Me. I AM the LORD, and
there is no other. There is no God besides Me. I will gird
you, though you have not known Me. That they may know
from the rising of the sun to its setting that there is none
besides Me. I AM the LORD, and there is no other.*

Isaiah 45:4-6 NKJV

*God didn't set us up for an angry rejection but for
salvation by Jesus Christ. He died for us, a death that
triggered life. Whether we're awake with the living or
asleep with the dead, we're alive with Him! O speak
encouraging words to one another. Build up hope so
you'll all be together in this, no one left out, no- one left
behind. I know you're already doing this; just keep on
doing it.*

1 Thessalonians 5:9-11 THE MESSAGE

*Don't become partners with those who reject God. How
can you make a partnership out of right and wrong?
That's not partnership; that's war. Is light best friends
with dark? Does Christ go strolling with the devil? Do*

trust and mistrust hold hands? Who would think of setting up pagan idols in God's holy Temple? But that is exactly what we are, each of us a temple in whom God lives. God Himself put it this way: 'I'll live in them, move into them; I'll be their God and they'll be My people. So leave the corruption and compromise; leave it for good', says God. 'Don't link up with those who will pollute you. I want you all for Myself. I'll be a Father to you; you'll be sons and daughters to Me.'

2 Corinthians 6:14-18 THE MESSAGE

...That is, that I may be encouraged together with you by the mutual faith both of you and me.

Romans 1:12 NKJV

Then the word of the LORD came to me saying: 'Before I formed you in the womb, I knew you; before you were born, I sanctified you...'

Jeremiah 1:4-5 NKJV

'Shout and be glad, O daughter [son] of Zion. For I AM coming, and I will live among you', declares the LORD.

Zechariah 2:10 NIV

Can two walk together, unless they are agreed?

Amos 3:3 NKJV

Gather yourselves together, yes, gather together...

Zephaniah 2:1 NKJV

For where two or three are gathered together in My Name, I AM there in the midst of them.

Matthew 18:20 NKJV

We ought always to thank God for you, brothers and sisters, and rightly so, because your faith is growing more and more, and the love all of you have for one another is increasing.

2 Thessalonians 1:3 NIV

So then, they are no longer two, but one flesh. Therefore what God has joined together, let not man separate.

Matthew 19:6 NKJV

...That their hearts may be encouraged, being knit together in love, and attaining to all riches of the full assurance of understanding, to the knowledge of the mystery of God...

Colossians 2:2 NKJV

Therefore, receive one another, just as Christ also received us, to the glory of God.

Romans 15:7 NKJV

That I may come to you with joy by the will of God, and may be refreshed together with you.

Romans 15:32 NKJV

Therefore be imitators of God as dear children, and walk in love, as Christ also has loved us and given Himself for us...

Ephesians 5:1-2 NKJV

Now I plead with you, brethren, by the Name of our Lord Jesus Christ, that you all speak the same thing, and that there be no divisions among you, but that you be perfectly joined together in the same mind and in the same judgment.

1 Corinthians 1:10 NKJV

For one will hardly die for a righteous man; though perhaps for the good man, someone would dare even to die. But God demonstrates His own love toward us, in that while we were yet sinners, Christ died for us.

Romans 5:7-8 NASB

O LORD, You have examined my heart and know everything about me. You know when I sit down or stand up. You know my thoughts even when I'm far away. You see me when I travel and when I rest at home. You know everything I do. You know what I am going to say even before I say it, LORD. You go before me and follow me. You place your hand of blessing on my head. Such knowledge is too wonderful for me, too great for me to understand! I can never escape from Your Spirit! I can never get away from Your presence! If I go up to heaven, You are there; if I go down to the grave, You are there. If I ride the wings of the morning, if I dwell by the farthest oceans, even there Your hand will guide me, and Your strength will support me. I could ask the darkness to hide me and the light around me to become night - but even in darkness I cannot hide from You. To You the night shines as bright as day. Darkness and light are the same to You. You made all the delicate, inner parts of my body and knit me together in my mother's womb. Thank You for making me so wonderfully complex! Your workmanship is marvelous - how well I know it. You watched me as I was being formed in utter seclusion, as I was woven together in the dark of the womb. You saw me before I was born. Every day of my life was recorded in Your book. Every moment was laid out before a single day had passed. How precious are Your thoughts about me, O God. They cannot be numbered! I can't even count them; they outnumber the grains of sand! And when I wake up, You are still with me!...Search me, O God, and know my heart; test me and know my anxious thoughts. Point out anything in me that offends You, and lead me along the path of everlasting life.

Psalm 139:1-18, 23-24 NLT

COURAGE

When I am intimidated or fearful and need to be bold

Be strong and of good courage. Do not fear nor be afraid of them; for the LORD your God, He is the One Who goes with you. He will not leave you nor forsake you.

Deuteronomy 31:6 NKJV

Have you not known? Have you not heard? The everlasting God, the LORD, the Creator of the ends of the earth, neither faints nor is weary. His understanding is unsearchable. He gives power to the weak, and to those who have no might He increases strength. Even the youths shall faint and be weary, and the young men shall utterly fall, but those who wait on the LORD shall renew their strength; they shall mount up with wings like eagles, they shall run and not be weary, they shall walk and not faint.

Isaiah 40:28-31 NKJV

I can do all things through Christ, Who strengthens me.

Philippians 4:13 NKJV

Fear not, for I AM with you; be not dismayed, for I AM your God. I will strengthen you, yes I will help you, I will uphold you with My righteous right hand. Behold all those who were incensed against you shall be ashamed and disgraced; they shall be as nothing and those who strive with you shall perish. You shall seek them and not find them – those who contended with you. Those who war against you shall be as nothing, as a nonexistent thing. For I, the LORD, your God, will hold your right hand, saying to you, 'Fear not, I will help you.'

Isaiah 41:10-15 NKJV

'They will fight against you, but they shall not prevail against you, for I AM with you,' says the LORD.

Jeremiah 1:19 NKJV

Do not be afraid, but speak and do not keep silent, for I AM with you, and no one will attack you to hurt you, for I have many people in this city.

Acts 18:10 NKJV

There is no fear in love; but perfect love casts out fear because fear involves torment.

1 John 4:18 NKJV

For God has not given us a spirit of fear, but of power and of love and of a sound mind.

2 Timothy 1:7 NKJV

I've commanded you to be strong and brave. Don't ever be afraid or discouraged! I AM the LORD your God, and I will be there to help you wherever you go.

Joshua 1:9 CEV

So we may boldly say: 'The LORD is my helper; I will not fear. What can man do to me?'

Hebrews 13:6 NKJV

Then said I, 'Oh, LORD God! Behold, I cannot speak, for I am a youth.' But the LORD said to me: 'Do not say I am a youth, for you shall go to all to whom I send you, and whatever I command you, you shall speak. Do not be afraid of their faces, for I AM with you to deliver you,' says the LORD.

Jeremiah 1:6-8 NKJV

Love God, all you saints; God takes care of all who stay close to Him, but He pays back in full those arrogant enough to go it alone. Be brave. Be strong. Don't give up. Expect God to get here soon.

Psalm 31:23-24 THE MESSAGE

Be of good courage, and let us be strong for our people and for the cities of our God. And may the LORD do what is good in His sight.

2 Samuel 10:12 NKJV

Who is going to harm you if you are eager to do good? But even if you should suffer for what is right, you are blessed. Do not fear what they fear; do not be frightened. But in your hearts set apart Christ as Lord. Always be prepared to give an answer to everyone who asks you to give the reason for the hope that you have. But do this with gentleness and respect, keeping a clear conscience, so that those who speak maliciously against your good behavior in Christ may be ashamed of their slander. It is better, if it is God's will, to suffer for doing good than for doing evil.

1 Peter 3:13-17 NIV

Watch, stand fast in the faith, be brave, be strong.

1 Corinthians 16:13 NKJV

Watch on the LORD and be good courage, and He shall strengthen your heart...

Psalm 27:14 NKJV

The LORD is on my side; I will not fear. What can man do to me?

Psalm 118:6 NKJV

Do not be afraid of sudden terror, nor of trouble from the wicked when it comes; for the LORD will be your confidence, and will keep your foot from being caught.

Proverbs 3:25-26 NKJV

For He orders His angels to protect you wherever you go.

Psalm 91:11 NKJV

But thus says the LORD ...'for I will contend with him who contends with you, and I will save your children.'

Isaiah 49:25 NKJV

Then the Word of the LORD came to Jeremiah, saying 'Behold, I AM the LORD, the God of all flesh. Is there anything too hard for Me?'

Jeremiah 32:26 NKJV

Deliverance

When my enemies or the bondage of negative thoughts and lifestyles torment me

I have chosen you and have not cast you away. Fear not, for I AM with you. Be not dismayed, for I AM your God. I will strengthen you. Yes, I will help you. I will uphold you with My righteous right hand.

Isaiah 41:9-10 NKJV

Do not be afraid. Stand firm and you will see the deliverance the LORD will bring you today.

Exodus 14:13 NIV

I run for dear life to God, I'll never live to regret it. Do what You do so well; get me out of this mess and up on my feet.

Psalm 71:1 THE MESSAGE

He sent from above, He took me. He drew me out of many waters. He delivered me from my strong enemy, from those who hated me, for they were too strong for me. They confronted me in the day of my calamity, but the

LORD was my support. He also brought me out into a broad place. He delivered me because He delighted in me.

Psalm 18:16-19 NKJV

I AM the LORD your God, and I will rescue you from all your enemies.

2 Kings 17:39 CEV

You will not have to fight this battle. Take up your positions; stand firm and see the deliverance the LORD will give you...Do not be afraid; do not be discouraged. Go out to face them tomorrow, and the LORD will be with you.

2 Chronicles 20:17 NIV

Yes, and I will continue to rejoice, for I know that through your prayers and the help given by the Spirit of Jesus Christ, what has happened to me will turn out for my deliverance.

Philippians 1:19 NIV

I will instruct you and teach you in the way you should go; I will guide you with My eye.

Psalm 32:8 NKJV

No temptation has overtaken you except such as is common to man; but God is faithful, Who will not allow you to be tempted beyond what you are able, but with the temptation will also make the way of escape, that you may be able to bear it.

1 Corinthians 10:13 NKJV

My son, if sinners entice you, do not consent.

Proverbs 1:10 NKJV

Let the wicked fall into their own nets, while I escape safely.

Psalm 141:10 NKJV

Because He Himself suffered when He was tempted, He is able to help those who are being tempted.

Hebrews 2:18 NIV

And do not lead us into temptation, but deliver us from the evil one. For Yours is the kingdom and the power and the glory forever. Amen.

Matthew 6:13 NKJV

Watch and pray, lest you enter into temptation. The spirit indeed is willing, but the flesh is weak.

Matthew 26:41 NKJV

Yes, I'm full of myself – after all, I've spent a long time in sin's prison. What I don't understand about myself is that I decide one way, but then I act another, doing things I absolutely despise. So if I can't be trusted to figure out what is best for myself, and then do it, it becomes obvious that God's command is necessary. But I need something more! For if I know the law but still can't keep it, and if the power of sin within me keeps sabotaging my best intentions, I obviously need help! I realize that I don't have what it takes...It happens so regularly that it's predictable. The moment I decide to do good, sin is there to trip me up. I truly delight in God's commands, but it's pretty obvious that not all of me joins in that delight. Parts of me covertly rebel, and just when I least expect it, they take charge. I've tried everything and nothing helps. I'm at the end of my rope. Is there no one who can do anything for me? Isn't that the real question? The answer, thank God, is that Jesus Christ can and does. He acted to set things right in this life of contradictions where I want to serve God with all my heart and mind, but am pulled by the influence of sin to do something totally different...With the arrival of Jesus, the Messiah, that fateful dilemma's resolved. Those who enter into Christ's being-here-for-us no longer have to live under a continuous, low-lying black cloud. A new power is in operation. The Spirit of life in Christ, like a strong wind, has magnificently cleared the air, freeing you from a fated lifetime of brutal tyranny at the hands of sin and death.

Romans 7:14-18, 7:21, 8:1-2 THE MESSAGE

When He came to the place, He said to them, 'Pray that you may not enter into temptation.'

Luke 22:40 NKJV

Blessed is the man who endures temptation; for when he has been approved, he will receive the crown of life which the Lord has promised to those who love Him.

James 1:12 NKJV

Do not deprive each other except by mutual consent and for a time, so that you may devote yourselves to prayer. Then come together again so that Satan will not tempt you because of your lack of self-control.

1 Corinthians 7:5 NIV

Here's what I want you to do: find a quiet, secluded place so you won't be tempted to role-play before God. Just be there as simply and honestly as you can manage. The focus will shift from you to God, and you will begin to sense His grace.

Matthew 6:6 THE MESSAGE

Deliver me in Your righteousness, and cause me to escape; Incline Your ear to me, and save me.

Psalm 71:2 NKJV

*Let no one say when he is tempted, 'I am tempted by God',
for God cannot be tempted by evil, nor does He Himself
tempt anyone. But each one is tempted when he is drawn
away by his own desires and is enticed.*

James 1:13-14 NKJV

*Pay close attention, friend, to what your father tells you;
never forget what you learned at your mother's knee.
Wear their counsel like flowers in your hair, like rings on
your fingers. Dear friend, if bad companions tempt you,
don't go along with them. If they say - 'Let's go out and
raise some hell. Let's beat up some old man, mug some
old woman. Let's pick them clean and get them ready for
their funerals. We'll load up on top-quality loot. We'll
haul it home by the truckload. Join us for the time of your
life! With us, it's share and share alike!' Oh, friend, don't
give them a second look; don't listen to them for a
minute. They're racing to a very bad end, hurrying to
ruin everything they lay hands on. Nobody robs a bank
with everyone watching, yet that's what these people are
doing - they're doing themselves in. When you grab all
you can get, that's what happens: the more you get, the
less you are.*

Proverbs 1:8-19 THE MESSAGE

*A violent man entices his neighbor, and leads him in a
way that is not good.*

Proverbs 16:29 NKJV

*Those who live in the shelter of the Most High will find
rest in the shadow of the Almighty. This I declare about
the LORD: He alone is my refuge, my place of safety; He is
my God, and I trust Him. For He will rescue you from
every trap and protect you from deadly disease. He will
cover you with His feathers. He will shelter you with His
wings. His faithful promises are your armor and
protection. Do not be afraid of the terrors of the night,*

nor the arrow that flies in the day. Do not dread the disease that stalks in darkness, nor the disaster that strikes at midday. Though a thousand fall at your side, though ten thousand are dying around you, these evils will not touch you. Just open your eyes, and see how the wicked are punished. If you make the LORD your refuge, if you make the Most High your shelter, no evil will conquer you; no plague will come near your home. For He will order His angels to protect you wherever you go. They will hold you up with their hands so you won't even hurt your foot on a stone. You will trample upon lions and cobras; you will crush fierce lions and serpents under your feet! The LORD says, 'I will rescue those who love Me. I will protect those who trust in My Name. When they call on Me, I will answer; I will be with them in trouble. I will rescue and honor them. I will reward them with a long life and give them My salvation.'

Psalm 91 NLT

When you pass through the waters, I will be with you. And through the rivers, they shall not overflow you. When you walk through the fire, you shall not be burned. Nor shall the flame scorch you. For I AM the LORD, your God, and Holy One of Israel, your Savior...you have been honored, and I have loved you...fear not, for I AM with you.

Isaiah 43:2-4 NKJV

DIRECTION

When I am feeling lost and need God's guidance

Your Word is a lamp to my feet and light to my path.

Psalm 119:105 NKJV

Trust in the LORD with all your heart and lean not on your own understanding. In all you do, acknowledge Him and He will make your paths straight.

Proverbs 3:5-6 NASB

But when He, the Spirit of Truth comes, He will guide you into all the Truth; for He will not speak on His own initiative, but whatever He hears, He will speak; and He will disclose to you what is to come.

John 16:13 NIV

But be doers of the Word, and not hearers only, deceiving yourselves.

James 1:22 NKJV

I AM always with You; You hold me by my right hand. You guide me with Your counsel and afterward, You will take me into glory.

Psalm 73:23-24 NIV

Your statutes are wonderful, therefore I obey them. The unfolding of Your Words gives light, it gives understanding to the simple. I open my mouth and pant, longing for Your commands. Turn to me and have mercy on me, as You always do to those who love Your name. Direct my footsteps according to Your Word; let no sin rule over me. Redeem me from the oppression of men that I may obey Your precepts. Make Your face shine upon Your servant and teach me Your decrees...righteous are You, O LORD, and Your laws are right. The statues You have laid down are righteous; they are fully trustworthy.

Psalm 119:129-135, 137 NIV

Whoever guards his mouth and tongue keeps his soul from troubles.

Proverbs 21:23 NKJV

Now, my son, may the LORD be with you and give you success as you follow His directions...

1 Chronicles 22:11 NLT

I pondered the direction of my life and I turned to follow Your laws.

Psalm 119:59 NLT

By this all will know that you are My disciples, if you have love for one another.

John 13:35 NKJV

The humble He guides in justice, and the humble He teaches His way.

Psalm 25:9 NKJV

Blessed, happy, fortunate, prosperous and enviable is the man who walks and lives not in the counsel of the ungodly, following their advice, their plans and purposes, nor stands submissive and inactive in the path where sinners walk, nor sits down to relax and rest where the scornful and the mockers gather. But his delight and desire are in the law of the Lord, and on His law, the precepts, the instructions, the teachings of God, he habitually meditates, ponders and studies, by day and by night. And he shall be like a tree firmly planted and tended by the streams of water, ready to bring forth its fruit in its season; its leaf also shall not fade or wither; and everything he does shall prosper and come to maturity.

Psalm 1:1-3 AMP

And now, little children, abide in Him that when He appears, we may have confidence and not be ashamed before Him at His coming.

1 John 2:28 NKJV

Can mighty pine trees grow tall without soil? Can luscious tomatoes flourish without water? Blossoming flowers look great before they're cut or picked, but without soil or water they wither more quickly than grass. That's what happens to all who forget God – all their hopes come to nothing. They hang their life from one thin thread, they hitch their fate to a spider web. One jiggle and the thread breaks, one jab and the web collapses.

Job 8:11-15 THE MESSAGE

I will bless the LORD Who has given me counsel. My heart also instructs me in the night seasons. I have set the LORD always before me because He is at my right hand and I shall not be moved.

Psalm 16:7-8 NKJV

Let your speech always be with grace, seasoned with salt, that you may know how you ought to answer each one.

Colossians 4:6 NKJV

Show me Your ways, O LORD; teach me Your paths. Lead me in Your truth and teach me, for You are the God of my salvation; on You I wait all the day.

Psalm 25:4-5 NKJV

I will instruct you and teach you in the way you should go; I will guide you with My eye.

Psalm 32:8 NKJV

Cause me to hear Your loving kindness in the morning, for in You do I trust; cause me to know the way in which I should walk, for I lift up my soul to You.

Psalm 143:8 NKJV

If you extend your soul to the hungry and satisfy the afflicted soul, then your light will dawn in the darkness...the LORD will guide you continually, and satisfy your soul in drought and strengthen your bones; you shall be like a watered garden, and like a spring of water, whose waters do not fail.

Isaiah 58:10-11 NKJV

But seek first the kingdom of God and His righteousness, and all these things shall be added to you.

Matthew 6:33 NKJV

I AM the vine, you are the branches. He who abides in Me, and I in him, bears much fruit; for without Me you can do nothing.

John 15:5 NKJV

The righteous will be happy to see the wicked destroyed, and the innocent will laugh in contempt. They will say,

'See how our enemies have been destroyed. The last of them have been consumed in the fire.' Submit to God, and you will have peace; then things will go well for you. Listen to His instructions, and store them in your heart. If you return to the Almighty, you will be restored - so clean up your life. If you give up your lust for money and throw your precious gold into the river, the Almighty Himself will be your treasure. He will be your precious silver! Then you will take delight in the Almighty and look up to God. You will pray to Him, and He will hear you, and you will fulfill your vows to Him. You will succeed in whatever you choose to do, and light will shine on the road ahead of you. If people are in trouble and you say, 'Help them,' God will save them. Even sinners will be rescued; they will be rescued because Your hands are pure.

Job 22: 19-30 NLT

It's a mark of good character to avert quarrels, but fools love to pick fights.

Proverbs 20:3 THE MESSAGE

Love and truth form a good leader; sound leadership is founded on loving integrity.

Proverbs 20:28 THE MESSAGE

If our minds are ruled by our desires, we will die. But if our minds are ruled by the Spirit, we will have life and peace.

Romans 8:6 CEV

For though we live in the world, we do not wage war as the world does. The weapons we fight with are not the weapons of the world. On the contrary, they have divine power to demolish strongholds. We demolish arguments and every pretension that sets itself up against the knowledge of God, and we take captive every thought to make it obedient to Christ.

2 Corinthians 10:3-5 NIV

Wicked souls love to make trouble; they feel nothing for friends and neighbors.

Proverbs 21:10 THE MESSAGE

DISCERNMENT

When I need clarity in my situation to make healthier choices

For the Word of God is living and powerful, and sharper than any two edged sword, piercing even to the division of soul and spirit, and of joints and marrow, and is a discerner of the thoughts and intents of the heart.

Hebrews 4:12 NKJV

Finally, brethren, whatever is true, whatever is honorable, whatever is right, whatever is pure, whatever is lovely, whatever is of good repute, if there is any excellence and if anything worthy of praise, dwell on these things. The things you have learned and received and heard and seen in me, practice these things, and the God of peace will be with you.

Philippians 4:8-9 NASB

He who guards his mouth preserves his life, but he who opens wide his lips shall have destruction.

Proverbs 13:3 NKJV

But put on the Lord Jesus Christ, and make no provision for the flesh, to fulfill its lusts.

Romans 13:14 NKJV

It wasn't so long ago that we ourselves were stupid and stubborn, dupes of sin, ordered every which way by our glands, going around with a chip on our shoulder, hated and hating back. But when God, our kind and loving Savior God, stepped in, He saved us from all that. It was all His doing; we had nothing to do with it. He gave us a good bath, and we came out of it new people, washed inside and out by the Holy Spirit. Our Savior Jesus poured out new life so generously. God's gift has restored our relationship with Him and given us back our lives. And there's more life to come - an eternity of life! You can count on this. I want you to put your foot down. Take a firm stand on these matters so that those who have put their trust in God will concentrate on the essentials that are good for everyone. Stay away from mindless, pointless quarrelling over genealogies and fine print in the law code. That gets you nowhere. Warn a quarrelsome person once or twice, but then be done with him. It's obvious that such a person is out of line, rebellious against God. By persisting in divisiveness he cuts himself off.

Titus 3:8-11 THE MESSAGE

Then you shall again discern between the righteous and the wicked, between one who serves God and one who does not serve Him.

Malachi 3:18 NKJV

My son, if you receive my words, and treasure my commands within you, so that you incline your ear to wisdom, and apply your heart to understanding; yes, if you cry out for discernment, and lift up your voice for understanding, if you seek her as silver, and search for her as for hidden treasures; then you will understand the fear of the LORD, and find the knowledge of God. For the LORD gives wisdom; from His mouth come knowledge and understanding; He stores up sound wisdom for the upright; He is a shield to those who walk uprightly; He guards the paths of justice, and preserves the way of His saints. Then you will understand righteousness and justice, equity and every good path. When wisdom enters your heart, and knowledge is pleasant to your soul, discretion will preserve you; understanding will keep you, to deliver you from the way of evil, from the man who speaks perverse things, from those who leave the paths of uprightness to walk in the ways of darkness; who rejoice in doing evil, and delight in the perversity of the wicked; whose ways are crooked, and who are devious in their paths; to deliver you from the immoral woman, from the seductress who flatters with her words, who forsakes the companion of her youth, and forgets the covenant of her God. For her house leads down to death, and her paths to the dead; none who go to her return, nor do they regain the paths of life - so you may walk in the way of goodness, and keep to the paths of righteousness. For the upright will dwell in the land, and the blameless will remain in it; but the wicked will be cut off from the earth, and the unfaithful will be uprooted from it.

Proverbs 2 NKJV

Intelligent children make their parents proud; lazy students embarrass their parents. The empty-headed treat life as a plaything; the perceptive grasp its meaning and make a go of it. Refuse good advice and watch your plans fail; take good counsel and watch them succeed.

Proverbs 15:20-22 THE MESSAGE

Therefore give to Your servant an understanding heart to judge Your people, that I may discern between good and evil. The Lord was pleased that Solomon had asked for [wisdom]. So God said to him, 'Since you have asked for this and not for long life or wealth for yourself, nor have asked for the death of your enemies but for discernment in administering justice, I will do what you have asked. I will give you a wise and discerning heart, so that there will never have been anyone like you, nor will there ever be.'

1 Kings 3:9, 11-12 NIV

And this I pray, that your love may abound still more and more in knowledge and all discernment.

Philippians 1:9 NKJV

And they shall teach My people the difference between the holy and the unholy, and cause them to discern between the unclean and the clean.

Ezekiel 44:23 NKJV

Dear friend, guard clear thinking and common sense with your life. Don't for a minute lose sight of them. They'll keep your soul alive and well, they'll keep you fit and attractive. You'll travel safely, you'll neither tire nor trip; you'll take afternoon naps without a worry, and you'll enjoy a good night's sleep. No need to panic over alarms or surprises, or predictions that doomsday's just around the corner. Because God will be right there with you, He'll keep you safe and sound.

Proverbs 3:21-26 THE MESSAGE

DISCIPLESHIP

When I need instruction to live a fruitful life

But don't, dear friend, resent God's discipline; don't sulk under His loving correction. It's the child He loves that God corrects; a father's delight is behind all this.

Proverbs 3:11-12 THE MESSAGE

The Scriptures train God's servants to do all kinds of good deeds.

2 Timothy 3:17 CEV

But I discipline my body and bring it into subjection, lest, when I have preached to others, I myself should become disqualified.

1 Corinthians 9:27 NKJV

Are students better than their teacher? But when they are fully trained, they will be like their teacher.

Luke 6:40 CEV

Let the peace of Christ keep you in tune with each other, in step with each other. None of this going off and doing your own thing, and cultivate thankfulness. Let the Word of Christ - the Message - have the run of the house. Give it plenty of room in your lives. Instruct and direct one another using good common sense. And sing, sing your hearts out to God! Let every detail in your lives - words, actions, whatever - be done in the name of the Master, Jesus, thanking God the Father every step of the way.

Colossians 3:15 THE MESSAGE

Apply your heart to instruction and your ears to words of knowledge. Do not withhold discipline from a child; if you punish him with a rod, he will not die. Punish him with the rod and save his soul from death. My son, if your heart is wise, then my heart will be glad; my inmost being will rejoice when your lips speak what is right. Do not let your heart envy sinners, but always be zealous for the fear of the LORD. There is surely a future hope for you, and your hope will not be cut off.

Proverbs 23:12-18 NIV

Ezra had spent his entire life studying and obeying the Law of the LORD and teaching it to others.

Ezra 7:10 CEV

And so, dear brothers and sisters, I plead with you to give your bodies to God because of all He has done for you. Let them be a living and holy sacrifice - the kind He will find acceptable. This is truly the way to worship Him. Don't copy the behavior and customs of this world, but let God transform you into a new person by changing the way you think. Then you will learn to know God's will for you, which is good and pleasing and perfect. Because of the privilege and authority God has given me, I give each of you this warning: don't think you are better than you really are. Be honest in your evaluation of yourselves, measuring yourselves by the faith God has given us. Just as our bodies have many parts and each part has a special function, so it is with Christ's body. We are many parts of one body, and we all belong to each other. In His grace, God has given us different gifts for doing certain things well. So if God has given you the ability to prophesy, speak out with as much faith as God has given you. If your gift is serving others, serve them well. If you are a teacher, teach well. If your gift is to encourage others, be encouraging. If it is giving, give generously. If God has given you leadership ability, take the responsibility seriously. And if you have a gift for showing kindness to others, do it gladly. Don't just pretend to love others. Really love them. Hate what is wrong. Hold tightly to what is good. Love each other with genuine affection, and take delight in honoring each other. Never be lazy, but work hard and serve the Lord enthusiastically. Rejoice in our confident hope. Be patient in trouble, and keep on praying. When God's people are in need, be ready to help them. Always be eager to practice hospitality. Bless those who persecute you. Don't curse them; pray that God will bless them. Be happy with those who are happy, and weep with those who weep. Live in harmony with each other. Don't be too proud to enjoy the company of ordinary people. And don't think you know it all! Never pay back evil with more evil. Do things in such a way that everyone can see you are honorable. Do all that you can to live in peace with everyone. Dear friends, never take revenge. Leave that to the righteous anger of God. For the Scriptures say, 'I will take revenge; I will pay them back,' says the LORD. Instead, if your enemies are hungry, feed them. If they are thirsty, give them something to drink....Don't let evil conquer you, but conquer evil by doing good.

Romans 12 NLT

And have you completely forgotten this word of encouragement that addresses you as a father addresses His son? It says, 'My son, do not make light of the Lord's discipline, and do not lose heart when He rebukes you, because the Lord disciplines the one He loves, and He chastens everyone He accepts as His son.' Endure hardship as discipline; God is treating you as His children. For what children are not disciplined by their father? If you are not disciplined - and everyone undergoes discipline - then you are not legitimate, not true sons and daughters at all. Moreover, we have all had human fathers who disciplined us and we respected them for it. How much more should we submit to the Father of spirits and live! They disciplined us for a little while as they thought best; but God disciplines us for our good, in order that we may share in His holiness. No discipline seems pleasant at the time, but painful. Later on, however, it produces a harvest of righteousness and peace for those who have been trained by it.

Hebrews 12:5-11 NIV

When You corrected me, it did me good because it taught me to study Your laws.

Psalm 119:71 CEV

ENCOURAGEMENT

When I am disappointed or disheartened and none of my efforts seem to make a difference

Though I walk in the midst of trouble, You will revive me. You will stretch forth Your hand against the wrath of my enemies and Your right hand will save me. The LORD will accomplish what concerns me; Your loving kindness, O LORD, is everlasting; Do not forsake the works of Your hands.

Psalm 138:7-8 NASB

I can do all things through Christ who strengthens me.

Philippians 4:13 NKJV

Then when he arrived and witnessed the grace of God, he rejoiced and began to encourage them all with resolute heart to remain true to the Lord; for he was a good man, and full of the Holy Spirit and of faith. And considerable numbers were brought to the Lord.

Acts 11:23-24 NASB

But they shook off the dust from their feet against them...and the disciples were filled with joy and with the Holy Spirit.

Acts 13:51-52 NKJV

I live by faith in the Son of God, Who loved me and gave Himself for me.

Galatians 2:20 NKJV

From the ends of the earth I call to You, I call as my heart grows faint; lead me to the Rock that is higher than I. For You have been my refuge, a strong tower against the foe.

Psalm 61:2-3 NIV

The God of our fathers has chosen you that you should know His will, and see the Just One, and hear the voice of His mouth. For you will be His witness to all men of what you have seen and heard.

Acts 22:14-15 NKJV

Plant your roots in Christ and let Him be the foundation for your life. Be strong in your faith, just as you were taught - and be grateful.

Colossians 2:7 CEV

My health may fail, and my spirit may grow weak, but God remains the strength of my heart; He is mine forever.

Psalm 73:26 NLT

If you can believe, all things are possible to him who believes.

Mark 9:23 NKJV

Anxiety in a man's heart weighs it down, but an encouraging word makes it glad.

Proverbs 12:25 AMP

Blessed is she who believed.

Luke 1:45 NKJV

Therefore submit to God. Resist the devil and he will flee from you.

James 4:7 NKJV

You now have sorrow, but I will see you again, and your heart will rejoice, and your joy no one will take from you.

John 16:22 NKJV

Wait on the LORD; be of good courage, and He shall strengthen your heart; wait, I say, on the LORD!

Psalm 27:14 NKJV

What marvelous love the Father has extended to us! Just look at it - we're called children of God! That's who we really are. But that's also why the world doesn't recognize us or take us seriously, because it has no idea Who He is or what He's up to. But friends, that's exactly who we are: children of God. And that's only the beginning.

1 John 3:1-2 THE MESSAGE

You have tested my heart. You have visited me in the night. You have tried me and found nothing. I have purposed that my mouth shall not transgress. Concerning the works of men, by the word of Your lips, I have kept away from the paths of the destroyer. Uphold my steps in Your paths, that my footsteps may not slip.

Psalm 17:3-5 NKJV

Have I not commanded you? Be strong and of good courage; do not be afraid, nor be dismayed, for the LORD your God is with you wherever you go.

Joshua 1:9 NKJV

Let not your heart be troubled; you believe in God, believe also in Me. In My Father's house are many mansions; if it were not so, I would have told you. I go to prepare a place for you. And if I go and prepare a place for you, I will come again and receive you to Myself, that where I AM; there you may be also.

John 14:1-3 NKJV

Love God, all you saints; God takes care of all who stay close to Him, but He pays back in full those arrogant enough to go it alone. Be brave. Be strong. Don't give up. Expect God to get here soon.

Psalm 31: 23-24 THE MESSAGE

The LORD repay your work, and a full reward be given you by the LORD God of Israel, under whose wings you have come for refuge.

Ruth 2:12 NKJV

But you shall receive power when the Holy Spirit has come upon you, and you shall be witnesses to Me...and to the end of the earth.

Acts 1:8 NKJV

In this you greatly rejoice, though now, for a little while, if need be, you have been grieved by various trials, that the genuineness of your faith, being much more precious than gold that perishes, though it is tested by fire, may be found to praise, honor, and glory at the revelations of Jesus Christ, Whom having not seen, you love.

1 Peter 1:6-8 NKJV

Now may the God of hope fill you with all joy and peace in believing, so that you will abound in hope by the power of the Holy Spirit.

Romans 15:13 NASB

This is the way God put it: They found grace out in the desert, these people who survived the killing. Israel, out looking for a place to rest, met God out looking for them!' God told them, 'I've never quit loving you and never will. Expect love, love, and more love! And so now I'll start over with you and build you up again...You'll resume your singing, grabbing tambourines and joining the dance. You'll go back to your old work of planting vineyards on the Samaritan hillsides, and sit back and enjoy the fruit - oh, how you'll enjoy those harvests!'

Jeremiah 31:2-6 THE MESSAGE

For with God nothing will be impossible.

Luke 1:37 NKJV

FAITH

When I question myself, or God, in the midst of difficulties

...faith comes by hearing, and hearing by the Word of God.

Romans 10:17 NKJV

Your faith has saved you. Go in peace.

Luke 7:50 NKJV

My message and my preaching were not with wise and persuasive words, but with a demonstration of the Spirit's power, so that your faith might not rest on men's wisdom, but on God's power.

1 Corinthians 2:4-5 NIV

So Jesus answered and said to them, 'Have faith in God.'

Mark 11:22 NKJV

...Who through Him believe in God, Who raised Him from the dead and gave Him glory, so that your faith and hope are in God.

1 Peter 1:21 NKJV

Faith is the confidence that what we hope for will actually happen; it gives us assurance about things we cannot see. Through their faith, the people in days of old earned a good reputation. By faith we understand that the entire universe was formed at God's command, that what we now see did not come from anything that can be seen.

Hebrews 11:1-3 NLT

Your mercies are new every morning; Great is Your faithfulness.

Lamentations 3:23 NKJV

Therefore know that the LORD your God, He is God, the faithful God who keeps covenant and mercy for a thousand generations with those who love Him and keep His commandments...

Deuteronomy 7:9 NKJV

Your mercy, O LORD, is in the heavens; Your faithfulness reaches to the clouds.

Psalm 36:5 NKJV

Now if God so clothes the grass of the field, which today is, and tomorrow is thrown into the oven, will He not much more clothe you, O you of little faith?

Matthew 6:30 NKJV

I will sing of the mercies of the LORD forever; with my mouth will I make known Your faithfulness to all generations. For I have said, Mercy shall be built up forever; Your faithfulness You shall establish in the very heavens.

Psalm 89:1-2 NKJV

To declare Your loving kindness in the morning and Your faithfulness every night...

Psalm 92:2 NKJV

Hear my prayer, O LORD, give ear to my supplications! In Your faithfulness answer me, and in Your righteousness.

Psalm 143:1 NKJV

A talebearer reveals secrets, but he who is of a faithful spirit conceals a matter.

Proverbs 11:13 NKJV

O LORD, You are my God. I will exalt You, I will praise Your Name, for You have done wonderful things; Your counsels of old are faithfulness and truth.

Isaiah 25:1 NKJV

Then behold, they brought to Him a paralytic lying on a bed. When Jesus saw their faith, He said to the paralytic, 'Son, be of good cheer; your sins are forgiven you.'

Matthew 9:2 NKJV

Then He said to the woman, 'Your faith has saved you. Go in peace.'

Luke 7:50 NKJV

And He said to her, 'Daughter, be of good cheer; your faith has made you well. Go in peace.'

Luke 8:48 NKJV

Then the disciples came to Jesus in private and asked, 'Why couldn't we drive [out the demons]?' He replied, 'Because you have so little faith. I tell you the truth, if you have faith as small as a mustard seed, you can say to this mountain, 'move from here to there,' and it will move. Nothing will be impossible for you.'

Matthew 17:20 NIV

When He saw their faith, He said to him, 'Man, your sins are forgiven you.'

Luke 5:20 NKJV

Woe to you, teachers of the law and Pharisees, you hypocrites! You give a tenth of your spices - mint, dill and cumin. But you have neglected the more important matters of the law - justice, mercy and faithfulness. You should have practiced the latter, without neglecting the former. You blind guides! You strain out a gnat but swallow a camel.

Matthew 23:23-24 NIV

His lord said to him, 'Well done, good and faithful servant; you were faithful over a few things, I will make you ruler over many things. Enter into the joy of your lord.'

Matthew 25:21 NKJV

But Jesus turned around, and when He saw her He said, 'Be of good cheer, daughter; your faith has made you well.' And the woman was made well from that hour.

Matthew 9:22 NKJV

Then He touched their eyes, saying, 'According to your faith let it be to you.'

Matthew 9:29 NKJV

For this child I prayed, and the LORD has granted me my petition which I asked of Him.

1 Samuel 1:27 NKJV

Whoever can be trusted with very little can also be trusted with much, and whoever is dishonest with very little will also be dishonest with much. So if you have not been trustworthy in handling worldly wealth, who will trust you with true riches? And if you have not been trustworthy with someone else's property, who will give you property of your own?

Luke 16:10-12 NIV

They preached the good news in that city and won a large number of disciples. Then they returned to Lystra, Iconium and Antioch, strengthening the disciples and encouraging them to remain true to the faith.

Acts 14: 21-22 NIV

So the churches were strengthened in the faith, and increased in number daily.

Acts 16:5 NIV

Then Jesus answered and said to her, 'O woman, great is your faith! Let it be to you as you desire.' And her daughter was healed from that very hour.

Matthew 15:28 NKJV

First, I thank my God through Jesus Christ for you all, that your faith is spoken of throughout the whole world.

Romans 1:8 NKJV

That Christ may dwell in your hearts through faith...being rooted and grounded in love...

Ephesians 3:17 NKJV

One Lord, one faith, one baptism.

Ephesians 4:5 NKJV

Therefore we conclude that a man is justified by faith apart from the deeds of the law.

Romans 3:28 NKJV

He did not waver at the promise of God through unbelief, but was strengthened in faith, giving glory to God.

Romans 4:20 NKJV

But He said to them, 'Where is your faith?' And they were afraid, and marveled, saying to one another, 'Who can this be? For He commands even the winds and water, and they obey Him!'

Luke 8:25 NKJV

Therefore, having been justified by faith, we have peace with God through our Lord Jesus Christ.

Romans 5:1 NKJV

For by grace you have been saved through faith, and that not of yourselves; it is the gift of God.

Ephesians 2:8 NKJV

No temptation has overtaken you except such as is common to man; but God is faithful, who will not allow you to be tempted beyond what you are able, but with the temptation will also make the way of escape, that you may be able to bear it.

1 Corinthians 10:13 NKJV

But that no one is justified by the law in the sight of God is evident, for the just shall live by faith.

Galatians 3:11 NKJV

Above all, taking the shield of faith with which you will be able to quench all the fiery darts of the wicked one.

Ephesians 6:16 NKJV

And being confident of this, I know that I shall remain and continue with you all for your progress and joy of faith...

Philippians 1:25 NKJV

But since we belong to the day, let us be self-controlled, putting on faith and love as a breastplate, and the hope of salvation as a helmet.

1 Thessalonians 5:8 NIV

How much more do I need to say? It would take too long to recount the stories of the faith of Gideon, Barak, Samson, Jephthah, David, Samuel, and all the prophets. By faith these people overthrew kingdoms, ruled with justice, and received what God had promised them. They shut the mouths of lions, quenched the flames of fire, and escaped death by the edge of the sword. Their weakness was turned to strength. They became strong in battle and put whole armies to flight. Women received their loved ones back again from death.

Hebrews 11:32-35 NLT

Favor

When I need breakthrough and heaven's help for a specific goal, focus, or season in life

For You, O LORD, will bless the righteous; with favor You will surround him as with a shield.

Psalm 5:12 NKJV

Instead of your shame, you shall have double honor. And instead of confusion they shall rejoice in their portion. Therefore in their land, they shall possess double; everlasting joy shall be theirs.

Isaiah 61:7 NKJV

For I will look on you favorably and make you fruitful, multiply you and confirm My covenant with you.

Leviticus 26:9 NKJV

Good understanding gains favor, but the way of the unfaithful is hard.

Proverbs 13:15 NKJV

Fools mock at sin, but among the upright there is favor.

Proverbs 14:9 NKJV

Let them shout for joy and be glad, who favor my righteous cause; and let them say continually, 'Let the LORD be magnified, who has pleasure in the prosperity of His servant.'

Psalm 35:27 NKJV

For You created my inmost being; You knit me together in my mother's womb. I praise You because I am fearfully and wonderfully made; Your works are wonderful. I know that full well.

Psalm 139:13-14 NIV

Who can find a virtuous wife? For her worth is far above rubies. The heart of her husband safely trusts her; so he will no lack of gain. She does him good and not evil all the days of her life as long as there is life within her.

Proverbs 31:10-12 NKJV

Indeed now, your servant has found favor in your sight, and you have increased your mercy which you have shown me by saving my life...

Genesis 19:19 NKJV

The LORD rewarded me according to my righteousness. According to the cleanness of my hands, He has recompensed me for I have kept the ways of the LORD, and have not wickedly departed from my God.

Psalm 18:20-21 NKJV

I humbly bow before you, that I may find favor in your sight, my lord, O king!

2 Samuel 16:4 NKJV

You have granted me life and favor and Your care has preserved my spirit.

Job 10:12 NKJV

He who earnestly seeks good finds favor, but trouble will come to him who seeks evil.

Proverbs 11:27 NKJV

For God gives wisdom and knowledge and joy to a man who is good in His sight; but to the sinner He gives the work of gathering and collecting, that He may give to him who is good before God.

Ecclesiastes 2:26 NKJV

For whoever finds Me finds life, and obtains favor from the LORD.

Proverbs 8:35 NKJV

This is how it is to be done; every creditor shall cancel any loan they have made to a fellow Israelite. They shall not require payment from anyone among their own people, because the LORD's time for cancelling debts has been proclaimed.

Deuteronomy 15:2 NKJV

For His anger is but for a moment, His favor is for life; weeping may endure for a night, but joy comes in the morning.

Psalm 30:5 NKJV

You did not choose Me, but I chose you and appointed you that you should go and bear fruit, and that your fruit should remain, that whatever you ask the Father in My Name, He may give you. These things I command you, that you love one another.

John 15:16-17 NKJV

So God can point to us in all future ages as examples of the incredible wealth of His grace and kindness toward us, as shown in all He has done for us who are united with Christ Jesus.

Ephesians 2:7 NKJV

Moreover whom He predestined, these He also called; whom He called, these He also justified; and whom He justified, these He also glorified. What then shall we say to these things? If God is for us, who can be against us? He who did not spare His own Son, but delivered Him up for us all, how shall He not with Him also freely give us all things? Who shall bring a charge against God's elect? It is God who justifies. Who is he who condemns? It is Christ who died, and furthermore is also risen, Who is even at the right hand of God, who also makes intercession for us. Who shall separate us from the love of Christ? Shall tribulation, or distress, or persecution, or famine, or nakedness, or peril, or sword? As it is written: 'For Your sake we are killed all day long; we are accounted as sheep for the slaughter.' Yet in all these things we are more than conquerors through Him who loved us. For I am persuaded that neither death nor life, nor angels nor principalities nor powers, nor things present nor things to come, nor height nor depth, nor any other created thing, shall be able to separate us from the love of God which is in Christ Jesus our Lord.

Romans 8:30-39 NKJV

A good man obtains favor from the LORD, but a man of wicked intentions He will condemn.

Proverbs 12:2 NKJV

You are of God, little children, and have overcome them because He who is in you is greater than he who is in the world.

1 John 4:4 NKJV

FORGIVENESS

When I feel ashamed of my mistakes or when my heart needs softening and compassion for others

If My people who are called by My Name will humble themselves, and pray and seek My face, and turn from their wicked ways, then I will hear from heaven, and will forgive their sin and heal their land.

2 Chronicles 7:14 NKJV

To the LORD our God belong mercy and forgiveness, though we have rebelled against Him.

Daniel 9:9 NKJV

Look around and take note...see if you can find one man, one woman, a single soul who does what is right and tries to live a true life. I want to forgive that person. This is God's decree.

Jeremiah 5:1-2 THE MESSAGE

And why do you look at the speck in your brother's eye, but do not consider the plank in your own eye? Or how can you say to your brother, 'let me remove the speck from your eye', and look, a plank is in your own eye? Hypocrite! First remove the plank from your own eye, and then you will see clearly to remove the speck from your brother's eye.

Matthew 7:3-5 NKJV

Since God chose you to be the holy people He loves, you must clothe yourselves with tender-hearted mercy, kindness, humility, gentleness, and patience. Make allowance for each other's faults, and forgive anyone who offends you. Remember, the Lord forgave you, so you must forgive others. Above all, clothe yourselves with love, which binds us all together in perfect harmony. And let the peace that comes from Christ rule in your hearts. For as members of one body you are called to live in peace. And always be thankful. Let the message about Christ, in all its richness, fill your lives. Teach and counsel each other with all the wisdom He gives. Sing psalms and hymns and spiritual songs to God with thankful hearts. And whatever you do or say, do it as a representative of the Lord Jesus, giving thanks through Him to God the Father.

Colossians 3:12-17 NLT

And forgive us our debts, as we forgive our debtors. For if you forgive men their trespasses, your heavenly Father will also forgive you.

Matthew 6:12, 14 NKJV

God makes everything come out right; He puts victims back on their feet... God is sheer mercy and grace; not easily angered, He's rich in love. He doesn't endlessly nag and scold, nor hold grudges forever. He doesn't treat us as our sins deserve, nor pay us back in full for our wrongs. As high as heaven is over the earth, so strong is His love to those who fear Him. And as far as sunrise is from sunset, He has separated us from our sins.

Psalm 103:12-16 THE MESSAGE

Look on my affliction and my pain, and forgive all my sins.

Psalm 25:18 NKJV

For You, LORD, are good, and ready to forgive, and abundant in mercy to all those who call upon You.

Psalm 86:5 NKJV

Then Peter came to Him and said, 'Lord, how often shall my brother sin against me, and I forgive him? Up to seven times?' Jesus said to him, 'I do not say to you, up to seven times, but up to seventy times seven.'

Matthew 18:21-22 NKJV

Let love be without hypocrisy. Abhor what is evil. Cling to what is good. Be kindly affectionate to one another with brotherly love, in honor giving preference to one another, not lagging in diligence, fervent, in spirit, serving the Lord, rejoicing in hope, patient in tribulation, continuing steadfastly in prayer, distributing to the needs of the saints, given to hospitality. Bless those who persecute you; bless and do not curse. Rejoice with those who rejoice, and weep with those who weep. Be of the same mind toward one another. Do not set your mind on high things, but associate with the humble. Do not be wise in your own opinion. Repay no one evil for evil. Have regard for good things in the sight of all men. If it is possible, as much as depends on you, live peaceably with all men. Beloved, do not avenge yourselves, but rather give place to wrath; for it is written 'vengeance is Mine, I will repay', says the Lord. Therefore, 'if your enemy is hungry, feed him; if he is thirsty, give him a drink; for in so doing, you will heap coals of fire on his head. Do not be overcome by evil, but overcome evil with good.'

Romans 12:9-21 NKJV

Then Jesus said, 'Father, forgive them, for they do not know what they do.'

Luke 23:34 NKJV

In Him we have redemption through His blood, the forgiveness of sins, according to the riches of His grace.

Ephesians 1:7 NKJV

If I speak with human eloquence and angelic ecstasy but don't love, I'm nothing but the creaking of a rusty gate. If I speak God's Word with power, revealing all his mysteries and making everything plain as day, and if I have faith that says to a mountain, 'Jump,' and it jumps, but I don't love, I'm nothing. If I give everything I own to the poor and even go to the stake to be burned as a martyr, but I don't love, I've gotten nowhere. So, no matter what I say, what I believe, and what I do, I'm bankrupt without love. Love never gives up. Love cares more for others than for self. Love doesn't want what it doesn't have. Love doesn't strut, doesn't have a swelled head, doesn't force itself on others, isn't always 'me first,' doesn't fly off the handle, doesn't keep score of the sins of others, doesn't revel when others grovel, takes pleasure in the flowering of truth, puts up with anything, trusts God always, always looks for the best, never looks back, but keeps going to the end. Love never dies. Inspired speech will be over some day; praying in tongues will end; understanding will reach its limit. We know only a portion of the truth, and what we say about God is always incomplete. But when the Complete arrives, our incompletes will be cancelled.

1 Corinthians 13 THE MESSAGE

For we do not have a High Priest who cannot sympathize with our weaknesses, but was in all points tempted as we are, yet without sin. Let us therefore come boldly to the throne of grace that we may obtain mercy and find grace to help in time of need.

Hebrews 4:15-16 NKJV

And be kind to one another, tender-hearted, forgiving one another, even as God in Christ forgave you.

Ephesians 4:32 NKJV

And whenever you stand praying, if you have anything against anyone, forgive him, that your Father in heaven may also forgive you your trespasses.

Mark 11:25 NKJV

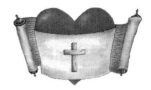

FRIENDSHIP

**To know Who my Best Friend truly is, and to build
relationships based on His example**

*Friends love through all kinds of weather, and families
stick together in all kinds of trouble.*

Psalm 17:17 THE MESSAGE

*To him who is afflicted, kindness should be shown by his
friend.*

Job 6:14 NKJV

*Above all things have fervent love for one another, for
love will cover a multitude of sins.*

1 Peter 4:8 NKJV

*My little children, let us not love in word or in tongue, but
in deed and in truth, and by this we know that we are of
the truth, and shall assure our hearts before Him.*

1 John 3:18-19 NKJV

*And let us consider how to give attentive, continuous care
to watching over one another, studying how we may stir
up, stimulate, and incite to love and helpful deeds and
noble activities, not forsaking or neglecting to assemble*

together as believers, as is the habit of some people, but admonishing, urging and encouraging one another, and all the more faithfully as you see the day approaching.

Hebrews 10:24-25 AMP

The seeds of good deeds become a tree of life; a wise person wins friends.

Proverbs 11:30 NLT

The Godly give good advice to their friends; the wicked lead them astray.

Proverbs 12:26 NLT

And be kind to one another, tender-hearted, forgiving one another, just as God in Christ forgave you.

Ephesians 4:32 NKJV

There are 'friends' who destroy each other, but a real friend sticks closer than a brother.

Proverbs 18:24 NLT

Whoever loves a pure heart and gracious speech will have the king as a friend.

Proverbs 22:11 NLT

For where two or three are gathered together in My Name, I AM there in the midst of them.

Matthew 18:20 NKJV

Don't walk around with a chip on your shoulder, always spoiling for a fight. Don't try to be like those who shoulder their way through life. Why be a bully?

Proverbs 3:30-31 THE MESSAGE

Strengthen your brethren.

Luke 22:32 NKJV

Bearing with one another, and forgiving one another, if anyone has a complaint against another, even as Christ forgave you, so you must do also.

Colossians 3:13 NKJV

Then Peter came to Him and said, 'Lord, how often shall my brother sin against me, and I forgive him? Up to seven times?' Then Jesus said to him, 'I do not say to you, up to seven times, but up to seventy times seven.'

Matthew 18:21-22 NKJV

Of course, your former friends are surprised when you no longer plunge into the flood of wild and destructive things they do. So they slander you.

1 Peter 4:4 NLT

Let us pursue things that make peace and things that edify another.

Romans 14:19 NKJV

But Jacob insisted, 'No, if I have found favor with you, please accept this gift from me. And what a relief to see your friendly smile. It is like seeing the face of God!'

Genesis 33:10 NLT

Be done with hypocrisy and jealousy and backstabbing...crave pure spiritual milk so that you can grow into the fullness of your salvation.

1 Peter 2:1-2 NLT

'Come over here and sit down, friend. I want to talk to you.' So they sat down together.

Ruth 4:1 NLT

The heartfelt counsel of friends is as sweet as perfume and incense. Never abandon a friend - either yours of your father's.

Proverbs 27:9-10 NLT

He whose walk is blameless and who does what is righteous, who speaks the truth from his heart and has no slander on his tongue, who does his neighbor no wrong and casts no slur on his fellowman, who despises a vile man but honors those who fear the LORD, who keeps his oath even when it hurts, who lends his money without usury and does not accept a bribe against the innocent. He who does these things will never be shaken.

Psalm 15:2-5 NIV

The LORD is a friend to those who fear Him. He teaches them His covenant.

Psalm 25:14 NLT

For the sake of my family and friends, I will say, 'May you have peace.'

Psalm 122:8 NLT

A friend is always loyal, and a brother is born to help in time of need.

Proverbs 17:17 NLT

An honest answer is like a kiss of friendship.

Proverbs 24:26 NLT

As iron sharpens iron, so a friend sharpens a friend.

Proverbs 27:17 NLT

Dear friends, since God loved us that much, we surely ought to love each other.

1 John 4:11 NLT

There is no greater love than to lay down one's life for one's friends. You are My friends if you do what I command. I no longer call you slaves, because a master doesn't confide in his slaves. Now you are My friends, since I have told you everything the Father told Me.

John 15:13-15 NLT

For since our friendship with God was restored by the death of His Son while we were still His enemies, we will certainly be saved through the life of His Son. So now we can rejoice in our wonderful new relationship with God because our Lord Jesus Christ has made us friends of God.

Romans 5:10-11 NLT

Dear friends, never take revenge. Leave that to the righteous anger of God. For the Scriptures say, 'I will take revenge; I will pay them back,' says the LORD.

Romans 12:19 NLT

Because we have these promises, dear friends, let us cleanse ourselves from everything that can defile our body or spirit. And let us work toward complete holiness because we fear God.

2 Corinthians 7:1 NLT

Why worry about a speck in your friend's eye when you have a log in your own? How can you think of saying to your friend, 'Let me help you get rid of that speck in your eye', when you can't see past the log in your own eye? You hypocrite! First get rid of the log in your own eye; then you will see well enough to deal with the speck in your friend's eye.

Matthew 7:3-5 NLT

Perhaps you think we're saying these things just to defend ourselves. No, we tell you this as Christ's servants, and with God as our witness. Everything we do, dear friends, is to strengthen you.

2 Corinthians 12:19 NLT

Therefore, my dear brothers and sisters, stay true to the Lord. I love you and long to see you, dear friends, for you are my joy and the crown I receive for my work.

Philippians 4:1 NLT

Never once did we try to win you with flattery, as you well know. And God is our witness that we were not pretending to be your friends just to get your money!

1 Thessalonians 2:5 NLT

So, my dear friends, flee from the worship of idols.

1 Corinthians 10:14 NLT

Dear friends, I warn you as 'temporary residents and foreigners' to keep away from worldly desires that wage war against your very souls.

1 Peter 2:11 NLT

Friends, when life gets really difficult, don't jump to the conclusion that God isn't on the job. Instead, be glad that you are in the very thick of what Christ experienced. This is a spiritual refining process, with glory just around the corner.

1 Peter 4:12-13 THE MESSAGE

Dear friends, let us continue to love one another, for love comes from God. Anyone who loves is a child of God and knows God.

1 John 4:7 NLT

But you, dear friends, must build each other up in your most holy faith, pray in the power of the Holy Spirit.

Jude 1:20 NLT

But you must not forget this one thing, dear friends: A day is like a thousand years to the Lord, and a thousand years is like a day...and so, dear friends, while you are waiting for these things to happen, make every effort to be found living peaceful lives that are pure and blameless in His sight. I am warning you ahead of time, dear friends. Be on guard so that you will not be carried away by the errors of these wicked people and lose your own secure footing.

2 Peter 3:8, 14, 17 NLT

I am writing to remind you, dear friends, that we should love one another. This is not a new commandment, but one we have had from the beginning.

2 John 1:5 NLT

Dear friend, you are being faithful to God when you care for the travelling teachers who pass through, even though they are strangers to you.

3 John 1:5 NLT

Dear friend, don't let [a] bad example influence you. Follow only what is good. Remember that those who do good prove that they are God's children, and those who do evil prove that they do not know God.

3 John 1:11 NLT

Look! I stand at the door and knock. If you hear My voice and open the door, I will come in, and we will share a meal together as friends.

Revelation 3:20 NLT

The way God designed our bodies is a model for understanding our lives together as a church: every part dependent on every other part, the parts we mention and the parts we don't, the parts we see and the parts we don't. If one part hurts, every other part is involved in the hurt, and in the healing. If one part flourishes, every other part enters into the exuberance.

1 Corinthians 12:25 THE MESSAGE

GENEROSITY

When I need to think of others more than myself

But this I say – he who sows sparingly will also reap sparingly, and he who sows bountifully will also reap bountifully. So let each one give as he purposes in his heart, not grudgingly or of necessity; for God loves a cheerful giver.

2 Corinthians 9:6-7 NKJV

If you see your enemy hungry, go buy him lunch; if he's thirsty, bring him a drink. Your generosity will surprise him with goodness, and God will look after you.

Proverbs 25:21 THE MESSAGE

Jesus did not come to be served but to serve and to give His life as a ransom for many.

Mark 10:45 NKJV

Don't pick on people, jump on their failures, criticize their faults - unless, of course, you want the same treatment. Don't condemn those who are down; that hardness can boomerang. Be easy on people; you'll find life a lot easier. Give away your life; you'll find life given back, but not merely given back—given back with bonus and blessing. Giving, not getting, is the way. Generosity begets generosity.

Luke 6:37-38 THE MESSAGE

You shall love your neighbor as yourself. Love does no harm to a neighbor, therefore love is the fulfillment of the law.

Romans 13:9-10 NASB

In the midst of a very severe trial, their overflowing joy and their extreme poverty welled up in rich generosity. For I testify that they gave as much as they were able, and even beyond their ability. Entirely on their own, they urgently pleaded with us for the privilege of sharing in this service to the saints. And they exceeded our expectations: they gave themselves first of all to the Lord, and then by the will of God also to us.

2 Corinthians 8:2-5 NIV

Listen carefully to what I am saying - and be wary of the shrewd advice that tells you how to get ahead in the world on your own. Giving, not getting, is the way. Generosity begets generosity. Stinginess impoverishes.

Mark 4:24-25 THE MESSAGE

And I am praying that you will put into action the generosity that comes from your faith as you understand and experience all the good things we have in Christ.

Philemon 1:6 NLT

If God so loved us, we also ought to love one another.

1 John 4:11 NKJV

Take a long, hard look. See how great He is - infinite, greater than anything you could ever imagine or figure out! He pulls water up out of the sea, distils it, and fills up his rain-cloud cisterns. Then the skies open up and pour out soaking showers on everyone. Does anyone have the slightest idea how this happens? How He arranges the clouds, how He speaks in thunder? Just look at that lightning, His sky-filling light show illumining the dark depths of the sea! These are the symbols of His sovereignty, His generosity, His loving care. He hurls arrows of light, taking sure and accurate aim. The High God roars in the thunder, angry against evil.

Job 36:26-28 THE MESSAGE

Command them to do good, to be rich in good deeds, and to be generous and willing to share.

1 Timothy 6:18 NIV

If someone says, 'I love God' and hates his brother, he is a liar; for he who does not love his brother whom he has seen, how can he love God whom he has not seen? And this commandment we have from Him; that he who loves God must love his brother also.

1 John 4:20-21 NKJV

Now we who are strong ought to bear the weaknesses of those without strength and not just please ourselves. Each of us is to please his neighbor for his good, to his edification. For even Christ did not please Himself...

Romans 15: 1-3 NASB

Providing honorable things, not only in the sight of the Lord, but also in the sight of men.

2 Corinthians 8:21 NKJV

One man gives freely, yet gains even more; another withholds unduly, but comes to poverty. A generous man will prosper; he who refreshes others will himself be refreshed.

Proverbs 11:24-25 NIV

So why are you now trying to out-god God, loading these new believers down with rules that crushed our ancestors and crushed us, too? Don't we believe that we are saved because the Master Jesus amazingly and out of sheer generosity moved to save us just as He did those from beyond our nation?

Acts 15:10-11 THE MESSAGE

For God is the one who provides seed for the farmer and then bread to eat. In the same way, He will provide and increase your resources and then produce a great harvest of generosity in you.

2 Corinthians 9:10 NLT

You will be enriched in every way so that you can be generous on every occasion, and through us your generosity will result in thanksgiving to God.

2 Corinthians 9:11 NIV

But now as for what is inside you - be generous to the poor, and everything will be clean for you.

Luke 11:41 NIV

He and all his family were devout and God-fearing; he gave generously to those in need and prayed to God regularly.

Acts 10:1-3 NIV

If any of you lacks wisdom, you should ask God, who gives generously to all without finding fault, and it will be given to you.

James 1:5 NIV

We have different gifts, according to the grace given to each of us. If your gift is prophesying, then prophesy in accordance with your faith, if it is serving, then serve; if it is teaching, then teach; if it is to encourage, then give encouragement; if it is giving, then give generously; if it is to lead, do it diligently; if it is to show mercy, do it cheerfully. Love must be sincere. Hate what is evil; cling to what is good. Be devoted to one another in love. Honor one another above yourselves. Never be lacking in zeal, but keep your spiritual fervor, serving the Lord. Be joyful in hope, patient in affliction, faithful in prayer. Share with God's people who are in need. Practice hospitality. Bless those who persecute you; bless and do not curse. Rejoice with those who rejoice; mourn with those who mourn. Live in harmony with one another. Do not be proud, but be willing to associate with people of low position. Do not be conceited. Do not repay anyone evil for evil. Be careful to do what is right in the eyes of everyone. If it is possible, as far as it depends on you, live at peace with everyone. Do not take revenge, my dear friends, but leave room for God's wrath, for it is written: 'It is Mine to avenge; I will repay,' says the Lord. On the contrary: 'If your enemy is hungry, feed him; if he is thirsty, give him something to drink.'

Romans 12:6-20 NIV

GRACE

When I need a second chance through God's amazing love for me

From the fullness of His grace we have all received one blessing after another...grace and truth came through Jesus Christ.

John 1:16-17 NIV

When he arrived and saw the evidence of the grace of God, he was glad and encouraged them all to remain true to the Lord with all their hearts.

Acts 11:23 NIV

I will greatly rejoice in the LORD. My soul shall be joyful in my God for He has clothed me with the garments of salvation. He has covered me with the robe of righteousness.

Isaiah 61:10 NKJV

Grace, God's undeserved favor, be with all who love our Lord Jesus Christ with undying and incorruptible Love.

Ephesians 6:24 AMP

So that being justified by His grace we would be made heirs according to the hope of eternal life.

Titus 3:7 NASB

In Him we have redemption through His blood, the forgiveness of sins, according to the riches of His grace.

Ephesians 1:7 NKJV

But He gives more grace. Therefore He says, 'God resists the proud, but gives grace to the humble.'...Humble yourselves in the sight of the Lord, and He will lift you up.

James 4:6, 10 NKJV

For everyone who exalts himself will be humbled, and he who humbles himself will be exalted.

Luke 14:11 NKJV

Now Stephen, a man full of God's grace and power, did great wonders and miraculous signs among the people.

Acts 6:8 NIV

...[We] are justified freely by His grace through the redemption that came by Christ Jesus.

Romans 3:24 NIV

But where sin increased, grace increased all the more...

Romans 5:20 NIV

For it is by grace you have been saved, through faith - and this not from yourselves, it is the gift of God.

Ephesians 2:8 NIV

Let your conversation be always full of grace, seasoned with salt, so that you may know how to answer everyone.

Colossians 4:6 NIV

All this is for your benefit, so that the grace that is reaching more and more people may cause thanksgiving to overflow to the glory of God.

2 Corinthians 4:15 NIV

For sin shall not be your master, because you are not under law, but under grace.

Romans 6:14 NIV

The God of peace will soon crush Satan under your feet. The grace of our Lord Jesus be with you.

Romans 16:20 NIV

Grace and peace to you from God our Father and the Lord Jesus Christ.

1 Corinthians 1:3 NIV

But just as you excel in everything - in faith, in speech, in knowledge, in complete earnestness and in your love for us - see that you also excel in this grace of giving... for you know the grace of our Lord Jesus Christ, that though He was rich, yet for your sakes He became poor, so that you through His poverty might become rich.

2 Corinthians 8:7, 9 NIV

And God is able to make all grace abound to you, so that in all things at all times, having all that you need, you will abound in every good work.

2 Corinthians 9:8 NIV

But He said to me, 'My grace is sufficient for you, for My power is made perfect in weakness.' Therefore I will boast all the more gladly about my weaknesses, so that Christ's power may rest on me.

2 Corinthians 12:9 NIV

May our Lord Jesus Christ Himself and God our Father, who loved us and by His grace gave us eternal encouragement and good hope.

2 Thessalonians 2:16 NIV

The grace of our Lord was poured out on me abundantly, along with the faith and love that are in Christ Jesus.

1 Timothy 1:14 NIV

GRATITUDE

To be thankful for all my blessings regardless of the circumstances

May the Lord Jesus Christ make you increase and abound in love to one another.

1 Thessalonians 3:12 NKJV

Because You have satisfied me, God, I promise to do everything You say. I beg You from the bottom of my heart: smile, be gracious to me just as You promised. When I took a long, careful look at Your ways, I got my feet back on the trail You blazed. I was up at once, didn't drag my feet, was quick to follow Your orders. The wicked hemmed me in - there was no way out - but not for a minute did I forget Your plan for me. I get up in the middle of the night to thank You; Your decisions are so right, so true - I can't wait till morning! I'm a friend and companion of all who fear You, of those committed to living by Your rules. Your love, God, fills the earth! Train me to live by Your counsel.

Psalm 119:57-64 THE MESSAGE

We boast about you, our God, and we are always grateful.

Psalm 44:8 CEV

It wasn't so long ago that you were mired in that old stagnant life of sin. You let the world, which doesn't know the first thing about living, tell you how to live. You filled your lungs with polluted unbelief, and then exhaled disobedience. We all did it, all of us doing what we felt like doing, when we felt like doing it, all of us in the same boat. It's a wonder God didn't lose His temper and do away with the whole lot of us. Instead, immense in mercy and with an incredible love, He embraced us. He took our sin-dead lives and made us alive in Christ. He did all this on His own, with no help from us! Then He picked us up and set us down in highest heaven in company with Jesus, our Messiah. Now God has us where He wants us, with all the time in this world and the next to shower grace and kindness upon us in Christ Jesus. Saving is all His idea, and all His work. All we do is trust Him enough to let Him do it. It's God's gift from start to finish! We don't play the major role. If we did, we'd probably go around bragging that we'd done the whole thing! No, we neither make nor save ourselves. God does both the making and saving. He creates each of us by Christ Jesus to join Him in the work He does, the good work He has gotten ready for us to do, work we had better be doing.

Ephesians 2:1-10 THE MESSAGE

Blessed be the name of God forever and ever, for wisdom and might are His, and He changes the times and the seasons; He removes kings and raises up kings; He gives wisdom to the wise and knowledge to those who have understanding. He reveals deep and secret things; and He knows what is in the darkness, and light dwells with Him. I thank You and praise You, O God of my fathers; You have given me wisdom and might, and have now made known to me what we asked of You, for You have made known to us the king's demand.

Daniel 2:20-23 NKJV

I'm so grateful to Christ Jesus for making me adequate to do this work. He went out on a limb, you know, in trusting me with this ministry. The only credentials I brought to it were invective and witch hunts and arrogance. But I was treated mercifully because I didn't know what I was doing - didn't know Who I was doing it against! Grace mixed with faith and love poured over me and into me. And all because of Jesus.

1 Timothy 1:12-14 THE MESSAGE

HEALING

When I need the tender touch of God, the Great Physician, for my heart, mind, soul, spirit, and body

'...I will restore health to you and heal you of your wounds,' says the LORD.

Jeremiah 30:17 NKJV

Behold, I will bring it health and healing: I will heal them and reveal to them the abundance of peace and truth.

Jeremiah 33:6 NKJV

I'll refresh tired bodies. I'll restore tired souls.

Jeremiah 31:25 THE MESSAGE

Then Your light shall break forth like the morning. Your healing shall spring forth speedily, and Your righteousness shall go before You. The glory of the LORD shall be your rear guard, then you shall call, and the LORD will answer. You shall cry, and He will say, 'Here I AM.'

Isaiah 58:8-9 NKJV

Let us draw near with a sincere heart in full assurance of faith, having our hearts sprinkled clean from an evil conscience and our bodies washed with pure water. Let us hold fast the confession of hope without wavering, for He Who promised is faithful.

Hebrews 10:22-23 NASB

But Jesus turned around, and when He saw her He said, 'Be of good cheer, daughter, your faith has made you well.' And the woman was made well from that hour.

Matthew 9:22 NKJV

Then Jesus said to him, 'Go your way: your faith has made you well.' And immediately, he received his sight and followed Jesus on the road.

Mark 10:52 NKJV

He forgives your sins - every one. He heals your diseases - every one. He redeems you from hell - saves your life! He crowns you with love and mercy - a paradise crown. He wraps you in goodness - beauty eternal. He renews your youth - you're always young in his presence.

Psalm 103:3 THE MESSAGE

Beloved, I pray that you may prosper in all things and be in health, just as your soul prospers.

3 John 1:2 NKJV

Jesus said, 'I'll come and heal him.'

Matthew 8:7 THE MESSAGE

A wicked messenger falls into trouble, but a faithful ambassador brings health.

Proverbs 13:17 NKJV

God's the One who rebuilds Jerusalem, Who re-gathers Israel's scattered exiles. He heals the heartbroken and bandages their wounds. He counts the stars and assigns each a name. Our Lord is great, with limitless strength; we'll never comprehend what He knows and does. God puts the fallen on their feet again and pushes the wicked into the ditch.

Psalm 147:2 THE MESSAGE

The king pleaded with the holy man, 'Help me! Pray to your God for the healing of my arm.' The holy man prayed for him and the king's arm was healed - as good as new!

1 Kings 13:6 THE MESSAGE

And He said to her, 'Daughter, be of good cheer; your faith has made you well. Go in peace.'

Luke 8:48 NKJV

Trust God from the bottom of your heart; don't try to figure out everything on your own. Listen for God's voice in everything you do, everywhere you go; He's the one who will keep you on track. Don't assume that you know it all. Run to God! Run from evil! Your body will glow with health, your very bones will vibrate with life! Honor God with everything you own; give Him the first and the best. Your barns will burst, your wine vats will brim over. But don't, dear friend, resent God's discipline; don't sulk under His loving correction. It's the child He loves that God corrects; a father's delight is behind all this.

Proverbs 3:5-12 THE MESSAGE

Kind words heal and help; cutting words wound and maim.

Proverbs 15:4 THE MESSAGE

When the woman realized that she couldn't remain hidden, she knelt trembling before Him. In front of all the people, she blurted out her story - why she touched Him and how at that same moment she was healed.

Luke 8:47 THE MESSAGE

A sound heart is life to the body, but envy is rottenness to the bones.

Proverbs 14:30 NKJV

The accumulated sorrows of your exile will dissipate. I, your God, will get rid of them for you. You've carried those burdens long enough. At the same time, I'll get rid of all those who've made your life miserable. I'll heal the maimed; I'll bring home the homeless. In the very countries where they were hated they will be venerated. On Judgment Day I'll bring you back home - a great family gathering! You'll be famous and honored all over the world. You'll see it with your own eyes - all those painful partings turned into reunions!

Zephaniah 3:18 THE MESSAGE

The light of the eyes rejoices the heart, and a good report makes the bones healthy.

Proverbs 15:30 NKJV

It is written, 'Man shall not live by bread alone, but by every word that proceeds from the mouth of God.'

Matthew 4:4 NKJV

There is one who speaks like the piercings of a sword, but the tongue of the wise promotes health.

Proverbs 12:18 NKJV

Pleasant words are like a honeycomb, sweetness to the soul and health to the bones.

Proverbs 16:24 NKJV

From there He went all over Galilee. He used synagogues for meeting places and taught people the truth of God. God's kingdom was His theme – that beginning right now they were under God's government, a good government! He also healed people of their diseases and of the bad effects of their bad lives. Word got around the entire Roman province of Syria. People brought anybody with an ailment, whether mental, emotional, or physical. Jesus healed them, one and all. More and more people came, the momentum gathering.

Matthew 4:23 THE MESSAGE

Then Jesus made a circuit of all the towns and villages. He taught in their meeting places, reported kingdom news, and healed their diseased bodies, healed their bruised and hurt lives. When He looked out over the crowds, His heart broke. So confused and aimless they were, like sheep with no shepherd. 'What a huge harvest!' He said to His disciples. 'How few workers! On your knees and pray for harvest hands!'

Matthew 9:35-38 THE MESSAGE

Jesus said to her, 'Daughter, you took a risk of faith, and now you're healed and whole. Live well, live blessed! Be healed of your plague.'

Mark 5:34 THE MESSAGE

I pray for good fortune in everything you do, and for your good health—that your everyday affairs prosper, as well as your soul! I was most happy when some friends arrived and brought the news that you persist in following the way of Truth. Nothing could make me happier than getting reports that my children continue diligently in the way of Truth!

3 John 1:1 THE MESSAGE

Jesus sent His twelve harvest hands out with this charge: 'Don't begin by traveling to some far-off place to convert unbelievers. And don't try to be dramatic by tackling some public enemy. Go to the lost, confused people right here in the neighborhood Tell them that the kingdom is here. Bring health to the sick. Raise the dead. Touch the untouchables. Kick out the demons. You have been treated generously, so live generously.'

Matthew 10:5-8 THE MESSAGE

We take our lead from Christ, Who is the source of everything we do. He keeps us in step with each other. His very breath and blood flow through us, nourishing us so that we will grow up healthy in God, robust in love.

Ephesians 4:16 THE MESSAGE

Hope

When I am feeling desperate or lost and need to remember God's promises and timing are perfect

Now may the God of hope fill you with all joy and peace in believing, that you may abound in hope by the power of the Holy Spirit.

Romans 15:13 NKJV

In the beginning, God created the heavens and the earth...

Genesis 1:1 NKJV

Peace I leave with you, My peace I give to you; not as the world gives do I give to you. Let not your heart be troubled, neither let it be afraid.

John 14:27 NKJV

I AM the light of the world.

John 8:12 NKJV

You'll be built solid, grounded in righteousness, far from any trouble – nothing to fear! Far from terror – it won't even come close! If anyone attacks you, don't for a moment suppose that I sent them, and if any should attack, nothing will come of it.

Isaiah 54:14-15 THE MESSAGE

God is light and in Him, there is no darkness at all.

1 John 1:5 NKJV

Let not your heart be troubled; you believe in God, believe also in Me.

John 14: 1 NKJV

I AM the way, the truth, and the life. No one comes to the Father except through Me.

John 14:6 NKJV

Beloved, do not think it strange concerning the fiery trial which is to try you, as though some strange thing happened to you, but rejoice to the extent that you partake of Christ's sufferings, that when His glory is revealed, you may also be glad with exceeding joy.

1 Peter 4:12-13 NKJV

But He saves the needy from the sword, from the mouth of the mighty, and from their hand. So the poor have hope, and injustice shuts her mouth.

Job 5:15-16 NKJV

What a God we have! And how fortunate we are to have Him, this Father of our Master Jesus! Because Jesus was raised from the dead, we've been given a brand-new life and have everything to live for, including a future in heaven - and the future starts now! God is keeping careful watch over us and the future. The Day is coming when you'll have it all - life healed and whole.

1 Peter 1:3-5 THE MESSAGE

The LORD is my shepherd. I shall not want. He makes me to lie down in green pastures. He leads me beside the still waters. He restores my soul. He leads me in the paths of righteousness for His Name's sake. Yea, though I walk through the valley of the shadow of death, I will fear no evil, for You are with me. Your rod and Your staff, they comfort me. You prepare a table before me in the presence of my enemies. You anoint my head with oil. My cup runs over. Surely goodness and mercy shall follow me all the days of my life, and I will dwell in the house of the LORD forever.

Psalm 23 NKJV

Therefore my heart is glad, and my glory rejoices; My flesh also will rest in hope.

Psalm 16:9 NKJV

I will visit you and perform My good word towards you, and cause you to return to this place. For I know the thoughts that I think toward you, says the LORD, thoughts of peace and not of evil, to give you a future and a hope. Then you will call upon Me and go and pray to Me, and I will listen to you. And you will seek Me and find Me, when you search for Me with all your heart. I will be found by you, says the LORD and I will bring you back from your captivity.

Jeremiah 29:10-14 NIV

Be of good courage, and He shall strengthen your heart, all you who hope in the LORD.

Psalm 31:24 NKJV

For You are my hope, O LORD God; You are my trust from my youth.

Psalm 71:5 NKJV

Why are you cast down, O my soul? And why are you disquieted within me? Hope in God; for I shall yet praise Him, the help of my countenance and my God.

Psalm 43:5 NKJV

For with God nothing is impossible.

Luke 1:37 NKJV

But I will hope continually, and will praise You yet more and more.

Psalm 71:14 NKJV

That they may set their hope in God, and not forget the works of God, but keep His commandments...

Psalm 78:7 NKJV

You are my hiding place and my shield; I hope in Your Word.

Psalm 119:114 NKJV

Uphold me according to Your Word, that I may live; and do not let me be ashamed of my hope.

Psalm 119:116 NKJV

Hope in the LORD; for with the LORD there is mercy, and with Him is abundant redemption.

Psalm 130:7 NKJV

Blessed is the man who trusts in the LORD, and whose hope is the LORD.

Jeremiah 17:7 NKJV

For I know the thoughts that I think toward you, says the LORD, thoughts of peace and not of evil, to give you a future and a hope.

Jeremiah 29:11 NKJV

...Rejoicing in hope, patient in tribulation, continuing steadfastly in prayer...

Romans 12:12 NKJV

Jesus answered and said to him, 'If anyone loves Me, he will keep My Word; and My Father will love him, and We will come to him and make Our home with him.'

John 14: 23 NKJV

This mystery has been kept in the dark for a long time, but now it's out in the open. God wanted everyone, not just Jews, to know this rich and glorious secret inside and out, regardless of their background, regardless of their religious standing. The mystery in a nutshell is just this: Christ is in you, so therefore you can look forward to sharing in God's glory. It's that simple. That is the substance of our Message. We preach Christ, warning people not to add to the Message. We teach in a spirit of profound common sense so that we can bring each person to maturity. To be mature is to be basic. Christ! No more, no less. That's what I'm working so hard at day after day, year after year, doing my best with the energy God so generously gives me.

Colossians 1:26-29 THE MESSAGE

Let us hold fast the confession of our hope without wavering, for He who promised is faithful.

Hebrews 10:23 NKJV

Just as rain and snow descend from the skies and don't go back until they've watered the earth doing their work of making things grow and blossom, producing seed for farmers and food for the hungry, so will the words that come out of My mouth – they will not come back empty handed. They will do the work I sent them to do, they'll complete the assignment I gave them.

Isaiah 55:11 THE MESSAGE

Most assuredly, I say to you, whatever you ask the Father in My Name, He will give you. Until now you have asked nothing in My Name. Ask, and you will receive, that your joy may be full.

John 16:23-24 NKJV

You will know the truth, and the truth will set you free.

John 8:32 NIV

All flesh is as grass, and all the glory of man, as the flower of the grass. The grass withers, and its flower falls away. But the Word of the Lord endures forever.

1 Peter 1:24-25 NKJV

And we know that all things work together for good to those who love God, to those who are the called according to His purpose.

Romans 8:28 NKJV

His lord said to him, 'Well done, good and faithful servant; you were faithful over a few things, I will make you ruler over many things. Enter into the joy of your lord.'

Matthew 25:23 NKJV

And Jesus came and spoke to them, saying, 'All authority has been given to Me in heaven and on earth. Go therefore and make disciples of all the nations, baptizing them in the Name of the Father and of the Son and of the Holy Spirit, teaching them to observe all things that I have commanded you. And lo, I AM with you always, even to the end of the age.' Amen.

Matthew 28:18-20 NKJV

These things I have spoken to you, that in Me you may have peace. In the world you will have tribulation; but be of good cheer, I have overcome the world.

John 16:33 NKJV

I pray that you will be grateful to God for letting you have part in what He has promised His people in the kingdom of light.

Colossians 1:12 CEV

You intended to harm me, but God intended it for good to accomplish what is now being done, the saving of many lives.

Genesis 50:20 NIV

Now hope does not disappoint, because the love of God has been poured out in our hearts by the Holy Spirit who was given to us.

Romans 5:5 NKJV

And my God will meet all your needs according to the riches of His glory in Christ Jesus.

Philippians 4:19 NKJV

Humility (Humbleness)

To be freed from the shackles of my insecurities and pride ("ego")

God resists the proud, but gives grace to the humble. Therefore humble yourselves under the mighty hand of God, that He may exalt you in due time, casting all your care upon Him, for He cares for you.

1 Peter 5:5-7 NKJV

'Don't let the wise brag of their wisdom. Don't let heroes brag of their exploits. Don't let the rich brag of their riches. If you brag, brag of this and this only – that you understand and know Me. I AM God and I act in loyal love. I do what's right and set things right and fair, and delight in those who do the same things. These are My trademarks.' God's decree.

Jeremiah 9:23-24 THE MESSAGE

But those who exalt themselves will be humbled, and those who humble themselves will be exalted.

Matthew 23:12 NLT

But as for me, I would seek God. And to God I would commit my cause – Who does great things, and unsearchable, marvelous things without number. He gives rain on the earth and sends waters on the fields. He sets on high those who are humble, and those who mourn are lifted to safety. He frustrates the devices of the crafty, so that their hands cannot carry out their plans. He catches them in their own craftiness, and the counsel of the cunning comes quickly upon them.

Job 5:8-13 NKJV

The humble He guides in justice. And the humble He teaches His way. All the paths of the LORD are mercy and truth, to such as keep His covenant and His testimonies. For Your Name's sake, O LORD, pardon my iniquity, for it is great. Who is the man that reveres the LORD? Him shall He teach in the way He chooses. He himself shall dwell in prosperity, and his descendants shall inherit the earth. The secret of the LORD is with those who revere Him, and He will show them His covenant.

Psalm 25:9-14 NKJV

Pride ends in humiliation, while humility brings honor.

Proverbs 29:23 NLT

For through the grace given to me I say to everyone among you not to think more highly of himself than he ought to think; but to think so as to have sound judgment, as God has allotted to each a measure of faith.

Romans 12:3 NASB

Let your gentleness be known to all men. The Lord is at hand.

Philippians 4:5 NKJV

Pride only breeds quarrels, but wisdom is found in those who take advice.

Proverbs 13:10 NIV

Beware that you do not forget the LORD your God by not keeping His commandments, His precepts, and His statutes which I command you today. Lest when you have eaten and are full, and have built Godly houses and live in them and when your herds and flocks multiply and your silver and gold is multiplied and all you have is multiplied. Then your minds and hearts be lifted up and you forget the LORD your God, Who brought you out of the land of Egypt, out of the house of bondage. Who led you through the great and terrible wilderness, with its fiery serpents and scorpions and thirsty ground, where there was no water, but Who brought you forth water out of the flinty rock, Who fed you in the wilderness with manna, which your fathers did not know, that He might humble you and test you, to do you good in the end. And beware lest you say in your mind and heart, 'my power and the might of my hand have gotten me this wealth.' But you shall earnestly remember the LORD your God, for it is He Who gives you power to get wealth, that He may establish His covenant which He swore to your fathers, as it is this day.

Deuteronomy 8:11-18 NKJV

Pride goes before destruction, a haughty spirit before a fall. Better it is to be of a humble spirit with the meek and poor than to divide the spoil with the proud. He who deals wisely and heeds God's word and counsel shall find good, and whoever leans on, trust in, and is confident in the Lord – happy, blessed and fortunate is he.

Proverbs 16:18-20 AMP

In his pride the wicked does not seek Him; in all his thoughts there is no room for God.

Psalm 10:4 NIV

Let the words of my mouth and the meditation of my heart be acceptable in Your sight, O LORD, my strength and my Redeemer.

Psalm 19:14 NKJV

Let their lying lips be silenced, for with pride and contempt they speak arrogantly against the righteous.

Psalm 31:18 NIV

I will not tolerate people who slander their neighbors. I will not endure conceit and pride.

Psalm 101:5 NLT

Pride leads to disgrace, but with humility comes wisdom.

Proverbs 11:2 NLT

But they, our ancestors, were arrogant; bull-headed, they wouldn't obey Your commands. They turned a deaf ear, they refused to remember the miracles You had done for them; They turned stubborn, got it into their heads to return to their Egyptian slavery. And You, a forgiving God, gracious and compassionate, incredibly patient, with tons of love - You didn't dump them. Yes, even when they cast a sculpted calf and said, 'This is your god who brought you out of Egypt,' and continued from bad to worse, You in your amazing compassion didn't walk off and leave them in the desert.

Nehemiah 9:16-19 THE MESSAGE

All who fear the LORD will hate evil. Therefore, I hate pride and arrogance, corruption and perverse speech.

Proverbs 8:13 NLT

First pride, then the crash—the bigger the ego, the harder the fall. It's better to live humbly among the poor than to live it up among the rich and famous. It pays to take life seriously; things work out when you trust in God.

Proverbs 16:18-20 THE MESSAGE

Finishing is better than starting. Patience is better than pride. Control your temper, for anger labels you a fool.

Ecclesiastes 7:8-9 NLT

Human pride will be brought down, and human arrogance will be humbled. Only the LORD will be exalted on that day of judgment.

Isaiah 2:11 NLT

I, the LORD, will punish the world for its evil and the wicked for their sin. I will crush the arrogance of the proud, and humble the pride of the mighty.

Isaiah 13:11 NLT

They will spread out their hands in it, as a swimmer spreads out his hands to swim. God will bring down their pride despite the cleverness of their hands.

Isaiah 25:11 NIV

'The terror you inspire and the pride of your heart have deceived you, you who live in the clefts of the rocks, who occupy the heights of the hill. Though you build your nest as high as the eagle's, from there I will bring you down,' declares the LORD.

Jeremiah 49:16 NIV

And the people...who spoke with such pride and arrogance, will soon know it.

Isaiah 9:9 NLT

The brother in humble circumstances ought to take pride in his high position.

James 1:9 NIV

He fed you with manna in the wilderness, a food unknown to your ancestors. He did this to humble you and test you for your own good.

Deuteronomy 8:16 NLT

You rescue the humble, but your eyes watch the proud and humiliate them.

2 Samuel 22:28 NLT

Then if My people who are called by My name will humble themselves and pray and seek My face and turn from their wicked ways, I will hear from heaven and will forgive their sins and restore their land.

2 Chronicles 7:14 NLT

He leads the humble in doing right, teaching them His way.

Psalm 25:9 NLT

To the faithful You show Yourself faithful; to those with integrity You show integrity. To the pure You show yourself pure, but to the wicked You show Yourself hostile. You rescue the humble, but You humiliate the proud.

Psalm 18:25-27 NLT

God, who has ruled forever, will hear me and humble them. For my enemies refuse to change their ways; they do not fear God.

Psalm 55:19 NLT

The humble will see their God at work and be glad. Let all who seek God's help be encouraged.

Psalm 69:32 NLT

The LORD said to my Lord, 'Sit in the place of honor at my right hand until I humble your enemies, making them a footstool under your feet.'

Psalm 110:1 NLT

Though the LORD is great, He cares for the humble, but He keeps His distance from the proud.

Psalm 138:6 NLT

The LORD supports the humble, but He brings the wicked down into the dust.

Psalm 147:6 NLT

For the LORD delights in His people; He crowns the humble with victory.

Psalm 149:4 NLT

The LORD mocks the mockers, but is gracious to the humble.

Proverbs 3:34 NLT

The humble will be filled with fresh joy from the LORD.

Isaiah 29:19 NLT

The Holy One, says this: 'I live in the high and holy place with those whose spirits are contrite and humble. I restore the crushed spirit of the humble and revive the courage of those with repentant hearts.'

Isaiah 57:15 NLT

My hands have made both heaven and earth; they and everything in them are Mine. I, the LORD, have spoken! I will bless those who have humble and contrite hearts...

Isaiah 66:2 NLT

Seek the LORD, all who are humble, and follow His commands. Seek to do what is right and to live humbly.

Zephaniah 2:3 NLT

God blesses those who are humble, for they will inherit the whole earth.

Matthew 5:5 NLT

Take My yoke upon you. Let Me teach you, because I AM humble and gentle at heart, and you will find rest for your souls.

Matthew 11:29 NLT

So anyone who becomes as humble as this little child is the greatest in the Kingdom of Heaven.

Matthew 18:4 NLT

But after Uzziah became powerful, his pride led to his downfall. He was unfaithful to the LORD his God.

2 Chronicles 26:16 NIV

He has brought down princes from their thrones and exalted the humble.

Luke 1:52 NLT

For those who exalt themselves will be humbled, and those who humble themselves will be exalted.

Luke 14:11 NLT

For Christ must reign until He humbles all His enemies beneath His feet.

1 Corinthians 15:25 NLT

INSPIRATION

When I feel unmotivated, insecure, or when I encounter ongoing obstacles

Delight yourself also in the LORD, and He shall give you the desires of your heart. Commit your way to the LORD, trust also in Him, and He shall bring it to pass.

Psalm 37:4-5 NKJV

Call to Me, and I will answer you and show you great and mighty things, which you do not know.

Jeremiah 33:3 NKJV

Are not two sparrows sold for a copper coin? And not one of them falls to the ground apart from your Father's will. But the very hairs of your head are all numbered. Do not fear therefore, you are of more value than many sparrows.

Matthew 10:29-31 NKJV

Then the word of the LORD came to Jeremiah, saying, 'Behold, I AM the LORD, the God of all flesh. Is there anything too hard for Me?'

Jeremiah 32:26 NKJV

Or do you not know that your body is the temple of the Holy Spirit who is in you, whom you have from God, and you are not your own? For you were bought at a price; therefore glorify God in your body and in your spirit, which are God's.

1 Corinthians 6:19-20 NKJV

If you're so smart, give us a lesson in how to address God. We're in the dark and can't figure it out. Do you think I'm dumb enough to challenge God? Wouldn't that just be asking for trouble? No one in his right mind stares straight at the sun on a clear and cloudless day. As gold comes from the northern mountains, so...beauty streams from God. 'Mighty God! Far beyond our reach! Unsurpassable in power and justice! It's unthinkable that He'd treat anyone unfairly. So bow to Him in deep reverence, one and all! If you're wise, you'll most certainly worship Him.'

Job 37:22-24 THE MESSAGE

For I am confident of this very thing that He who began a good work in you will perfect it until the day of Christ Jesus.

Philippians 1:6 NASB

Do you not know that you are the temple of God and that the Spirit of God dwells in you?

1 Corinthians 3:16 NKJV

My response is to get down on my knees before the Father, this magnificent Father who parcels out all heaven and earth. I ask Him to strengthen you by His Spirit—not a brute strength but a glorious inner strength—that Christ will live in you as you open the door and invite Him in. And I ask Him that with both feet planted firmly on love, you'll be able to take in with all followers of Jesus the extravagant dimensions of Christ's love. Reach out and experience the breadth! Test its length! Plumb the depths! Rise to the heights! Live full lives, full in the fullness of God. God can do anything, you know – far more than you could ever imagine or guess or request in your wildest dreams! He does it not by pushing us around but by working within us, His Spirit deeply and gently within us.

Ephesians 3:14-20 THE MESSAGE

Jesus Christ, the Messiah is always the same, yesterday, today, yes, and forever to the ages. Do not be carried about by different and varied and alien teachings; for it is good for the heart to be established and ennobled and strengthened by means of grace, God's favor and spiritual blessing, and not to be devoted to foods, rules of diet and ritualistic meals, which bring no spiritual benefit or profit to those who observe them.

Hebrews 13:8-9 AMP

Therefore, as the elect of God, holy and beloved, put on tender mercies, kindness, humility, meekness, longsuffering; bearing with one another, and forgiving one another, if anyone has a complaint against another; even as Christ forgave you, so you also must do. But above all these things put on love, which is the bond of perfection.

Colossians 3:12-14 NKJV

...that the God of our Lord Jesus Christ, the Father of glory, may give to you the spirit of wisdom and revelation in the knowledge of Him, the eyes of your understanding being enlightened; that you may know what is the hope of His calling, what are the riches of the glory of His inheritance in the saints and what is the exceeding greatness of His power toward us who believe, according to the working of His mighty power.

Ephesians 1:17-19 NKJV

He does great things past our finding out. Yes, wonders without number.

Job 9:10 NKJV

Then the righteous will shine forth as the sun in the kingdom of their Father. He who has ears to hear, let him hear!

Matthew 13:43 NKJV

Do not be afraid – only believe.

Mark 5:36 NKJV

'I, Wisdom, live together with good judgment. I know where to discover knowledge and discernment. All who fear the LORD will hate evil. Therefore, I hate pride and arrogance, corruption and perverse speech. Common sense and success belong to Me. Insight and strength are Mine. Because of Me, kings reign, and rulers make just decrees. Rulers lead with My help, and nobles make righteous judgments. I love all who love Me. Those who search will surely find Me. I have riches and honor, as well as enduring wealth and justice. My gifts are better than gold, even the purest gold, My wages better than sterling silver! I walk in righteousness, in paths of justice. Those who love Me inherit wealth. I will fill their treasuries.'

Proverbs 8:12-21 NLT

Is anyone thirsty? Come and drink - even if you have no money! Come, take your choice of wine or milk - it's all free! Why spend your money on food that does not give you strength? Why pay for food that does you no good? Listen to Me, and you will eat what is good. You will enjoy the finest food. Come to Me with your ears wide open. Listen, and you will find life. I will make an everlasting covenant with you. I will give you all the unfailing love I promised to David. See how I used him to display My power among the peoples. I made him a leader among the nations. You also will command nations you do not know, and peoples unknown to you will come running to obey, because I, the LORD your God, the Holy One of Israel, have made you glorious. Seek the LORD while you can find Him. Call on Him now while he is near. Let the wicked change their ways and banish the very thought of doing wrong. Let them turn to the LORD that He may have mercy on them. Yes, turn to our God, for He will forgive generously. 'My thoughts are nothing like your thoughts,' says the LORD. 'And My ways are far beyond anything you could imagine. For just as the heavens are higher than the earth, so My ways are higher than your ways and My thoughts higher than your thoughts.' The rain and snow come down from the heavens and stay on the ground to water the earth. They cause the grain to grow, producing seed for the farmer and bread for the hungry. It is the same with My word. I send it out, and it always produces fruit. It will accomplish all I want it to, and it will prosper everywhere I send it. You will live in joy and peace. The mountains and hills will burst into song, and the trees of the field will clap their hands! Where once there were thorns, cypress trees will grow. Where nettles grew, myrtles will sprout up. These events will bring great honor to the LORD's Name; they will be an everlasting sign of His power and love.

Isaiah 55 NLT

Joy

To celebrate and praise God for my life and all He's done for me

May the God of your hope so fill you with all joy and peace in believing through the experience of your faith that by the power of the Holy Spirit, you may abound and be overflowing and bubbling over with hope.

Romans 15:13 Amplified

So you'll go out in joy. You'll be led into a whole and complete life. The mountains and hills will lead the parade, bursting with song. All the trees of the forest will join the procession, exuberant with applause. No more thistles, but giant sequoias, no more thorn bushes, but stately pines – monuments to Me, to God, living and lasting evidence of God.

Isaiah 55:12-13 THE MESSAGE

Do not sorrow, for the joy of the LORD is your strength.

Nehemiah 8:10 NKJV

But let all those rejoice who put their trust in You. Let them ever shout for joy, because You defend them; let those also who love Your Name be joyful in You. For You,

O LORD, will bless the righteous; with favor, You will surround him as with a shield.

Psalm 5:11-12 NKJV

The king shall have joy in Your strength, O LORD. And in Your salvation how greatly shall he rejoice! You have given him his heart's desire and have not withheld the request of his lips. For You meet him with the blessings of goodness. You set a crown of pure gold upon his head. He asked life from You and You gave it to him. Length of days forever and ever. His glory is great in Your salvation. Honor and majesty, You have placed upon him. For You have made him most blessed forever. You have made him exceedingly glad with Your presence. For the king trusts in the LORD, and through the mercy of the Most High he shall not be moved.

Psalm 21:1-7 NKJV

I have great confidence in you; I take great pride in you. I am greatly encouraged; in all our troubles, my joy knows no bounds.

2 Corinthians 7:4 NIV

Mercy, peace, and love be multiplied to you.

Jude 1:2 NKJV

I will exalt You, my God and King, and praise Your Name forever and ever. I will praise you every day; yes, I will praise You forever. Great is the LORD! He is most worthy of praise! No one can measure His greatness. Let each generation tell its children of Your mighty acts; let them proclaim Your power. I will meditate on Your majestic, glorious splendor and Your wonderful miracles. Your awe-inspiring deeds will be on every tongue; I will proclaim Your greatness. Everyone will share the story of Your wonderful goodness; they will sing with joy about Your righteousness. The LORD is merciful and compassionate, slow to get angry and filled with unfailing love. The LORD is good to everyone. He showers compassion on all His creation. All of Your works will thank you, LORD, and Your faithful followers will praise You. They will speak of the glory of Your kingdom; they will give examples of Your power. They will tell about Your mighty deeds and about the majesty and glory of Your reign. For Your kingdom is an everlasting kingdom. You rule throughout all generations. The LORD always keeps His promises; He is gracious in all He does. The LORD helps the fallen and lifts those bent beneath their loads. The eyes of all look to You in hope; You give them their food as they need it. When You open your hand, You satisfy the hunger and thirst of every living thing. The LORD is righteous in everything He does; He is filled with kindness. The LORD is close to all who call on Him, yes, to all who call on Him in truth. He grants the desires of those who fear Him; He hears their cries for help and rescues them. The LORD protects all those who love Him, but He destroys the wicked. I will praise the LORD, and may everyone on earth bless His Holy Name forever and ever.

Psalm 145 NLT

I always thank my God as I remember you in my prayers, because I hear about your faith in the Lord Jesus and your love for all the saints. I pray that you may be active in sharing your faith, so that you will have a full understanding of every good thing we have in Christ. Your love has given me great joy and encouragement, because you, brother, have refreshed the hearts of the saints.

Philemon 1:4-7 NIV

Seize life! Eat bread with gusto, drink wine with a robust heart. Oh yes— God takes pleasure in your pleasure! Dress festively every morning. Don't skimp on colors and scarves. Relish life with the spouse you love each and every day... Each day is God's gift...Make the most of each one! Whatever turns up, grab it and do it. And heartily!

Ecclesiastes 9:7 THE MESSAGE

When the LORD brought back His exiles to Jerusalem, it was like a dream! We were filled with laughter, and we sang for joy. And the other nations said, 'What amazing things the LORD has done for them.' Yes, the LORD has done amazing things for us! What joy! Restore our fortunes, LORD, as streams renew the desert. Those who plant in tears will harvest with shouts of joy. They weep as they go to plant their seed, but they sing as they return with the harvest.

Psalm 126 NLT

Rejoice in the Lord always; again I will say rejoice! Let your gentle spirit be known to all men. The Lord is near.

Philippians 4:4-5 NASB

In every way, Christ is shared, and in this I rejoice.

Philippians 1:18 NKJV

KNOWLEDGE AND UNDERSTANDING

When I need God's Wisdom and revelation for my situation

The [reverence] of the LORD is the beginning of knowledge, but fools despise wisdom and instruction. The reverence of the LORD is the beginning of wisdom and the knowledge of the Holy One is understanding.

Proverbs 1:7, 9-10 NKJV

Therefore know this day, and consider it in your heart, that the LORD Himself is God in heaven above and on the earth beneath; there is no other.

Deuteronomy 4:39 NKJV

He who comes to Me will never hunger and he who believes in Me will never thirst.

John 6:35 NKJV

Let the Word of Christ dwell in you richly in all wisdom, teaching and admonishing one another in psalms and hymns and spiritual songs, singing with grace in your hearts to the Lord.

Colossians 3:16 NKJV

Now it is God who has made us for this very purpose and has given us the Spirit as a deposit, guaranteeing what is to come.

2 Corinthians 5:5 NIV

Search me, O God, and know my heart; test me and know my anxious thoughts. See if there is any offensive way in me, and lead me in the way everlasting.

Psalm 139:23-24 NIV

But the fruit of the Spirit is love, joy peace, longsuffering, kindness, goodness, faithfulness, gentleness, self-control. Against such there is no law.

Galatians 5:22-23 NKJV

Blessed is the man who trusts in the LORD, and whose hope is the LORD. For he shall be like a tree planted by the waters which spreads out its roots by the river, and will not fear when heat comes, but its leaf will be green and will not be anxious in the year of drought, nor will cease from yielding fruit.

Jeremiah 17:7-8 NKJV

Create in me a clean heart, O God, and renew a steadfast spirit within me.

Psalm 51:10 NKJV

Do not be carried away by all kinds of strange teachings. It is good for our hearts to be strengthened by grace, not by ceremonial foods, which are of no value to those who eat them.

Hebrews 13:9 NIV

'For even if the mountains walk away and the hills fall to pieces, My love won't walk away from you, My covenant commitment of peace won't fall apart.' The God who has compassion on you says so.

Isaiah 54:9 THE MESSAGE

For He satisfies the longing soul, and fills the hungry soul with goodness.

Psalm 107:9 NKJV

The LORD is near to all who call upon Him, to all who call upon Him in truth.

Psalm 145:18 NKJV

For God is not the author of confusion, but of peace, as in all the churches of the saints.

1 Corinthians 14:33 NKJV

Trust God from the bottom of your heart; don't try to figure out everything on your own. Listen for God's voice in everything you do, everywhere you go; He's the one who will keep you on track. Don't assume that you know it all. Run to God! Run from evil! Your body will glow with health, your very bones will vibrate with life! Honor God with everything you own; give Him the first and the best. Your barns will burst, your wine vats will brim over. But don't, dear friend, resent God's discipline; don't sulk under His loving correction. It's the child He loves that God corrects; a father's delight is behind all this.

Proverbs 3:5-12 THE MESSAGE

The LORD God has given me the tongue of the learned that I should know how to speak a word in season to him who is weary. He awakens me morning by morning. He awakens my ear to hear as the learned. The LORD God has opened my ear; and I was not rebellious, nor did I turn away.

Isaiah 50:4-5 NKJV

Show me Your ways, O LORD. Teach me Your paths. Lead me in Your truth and teach me for You are the God of my salvation. On You I wait all the day.

Psalm 25:4-5 NKJV

For where you have envy and selfish ambition, there you find disorder and every evil practice.

James 3:16 NIV

Be sober, be vigilant, because your adversary, the devil walks about like a roaring lion, seeking whom he may devour. Resist him, steadfast in the faith, knowing that the same sufferings are experienced by your brotherhood in the world. But may the God of all grace, who called us to His eternal glory by Christ Jesus, after you have suffered a while, perfect, establish, strengthen and settle you.

1 Peter 5:8-10 NKJV

'Let not the wise man glory in his wisdom, let not the mighty man glory in his might, nor let the rich man glory in his riches; but let him who glories, glory in this – that he understands and knows Me. That I AM the LORD, exercising loving kindness, judgment, and righteousness in the earth. For in these, I delight,' says the LORD.

Jeremiah 10:23-34 NKJV

I AM the Lord your God, Who brought you out of the land of Egypt, from the house of bondage. You shall have no other gods before Me or besides Me. You shall not make for yourself to worship a graven image or any likeness of anything that is in the heavens above or that is in the earth beneath or that is in the water under the earth. You shall not bow down to them or serve them; for I the Lord your God, AM a jealous God, visiting the iniquity of the fathers upon the children to the third and fourth generations of those who hate Me. And showing mercy and steadfast love to thousands and to a thousand generations of those who love Me and keep My commandments. You shall not take the Name of the Lord your God in vain, for the Lord will not hold him guiltless who takes His Name in falsehood or without purpose. Observe the Sabbath day to keep it holy, as the Lord your God commanded you. Six days you shall labor and do all your work. But the seventh day is a Sabbath to the Lord your God, in it you shall not do any work, you or your son or your daughter, or your manservant or your maidservant, or your ox or your donkey or any of your livestock, or the stranger or sojourner who is within your gates, that your manservant and your maidservant may rest as well as you. And earnestly remember that you were a servant in the land of Egypt and that the Lord your God brought you out from there with a mighty hand an outstretched arm; therefore the Lord your God commanded you to observe and take heed to the Sabbath day. Honor your father and your mother, as the Lord your God commanded you, that you days may be prolonged and that it may go well with you in the land with the Lord your God gives you. You shall not murder. Neither shall you commit adultery. Neither shall you act slyly or steal. Neither shall you witness falsely against your neighbor. Neither shall you covet your neighbor's wife, nor desire your neighbor's house, his field, his manservant or his maidservant, his ox, or his donkey, or anything that is your neighbor's. These words the Lord spoke to all you assembly on the mountain out of the midst of the fire, the cloud, and the thick darkness, with a loud voice; and He spoke not again, and added no more.

He wrote them on two tablets of stone and gave them to Moses.

Deuteronomy 5:6-22 AMP

For wrath kills a foolish man, and envy slays a simple one.

Job 5:2 NKJV

But where, oh where, will they find Wisdom? Where does Insight hide? Mortals don't have a clue - haven't the slightest idea where to look. Earth's depths say, 'It's not here'; ocean deeps echo, Never heard of it.' It can't be bought with the finest gold; no amount of silver can get it. Even famous Ophir gold can't buy it, not even diamonds and sapphires. Neither gold nor emeralds are comparable; extravagant jewelry can't touch it. Pearl necklaces and ruby bracelets - why bother? None of this is even a down payment on Wisdom! Pile gold and African diamonds as high as you will, they can't hold a candle to Wisdom. So where does Wisdom come from? And where does Insight live? It can't be found by looking, no matter how deep you dig, no matter how high you fly. If you search through the graveyard and question the dead, they say, 'We've only heard rumors of it.' God alone knows the way to Wisdom, He knows the exact place to find it. He knows where everything is on earth, He sees everything under heaven. After He commanded the winds to blow and measured out the waters, arranged for the rain and set off explosions of thunder and lightning. He focused on Wisdom, made sure it was all set and tested and ready. Then he addressed the human race: 'Here it is! [Honor and revere] the Lord - that's Wisdom, and Insight means shunning evil.'

Job 28:12-28 THE MESSAGE

If with heart and soul you're doing good, do you think you can be stopped? Even if you suffer for it, you're still better off. Don't give the opposition a second thought. Through thick and thin, keep your hearts at attention, in adoration before Christ, your Master. Be ready to speak up and tell anyone who asks why you're living the way you are, and always with the utmost courtesy. Keep a clear conscience before God so that when people throw mud at you, none of it will stick. They'll end up realizing that they're the ones who need a bath. It's better to suffer for doing good, if that's what God wants, than to be punished for doing bad. That's what Christ did definitively: suffered because of others' sins, the Righteous One for the unrighteous ones. He went through it all - was put to death and then made alive - to bring us to God.

1 Peter 3:13-18 THE MESSAGE

The secret things belong to the LORD our God, but those things which are revealed belong to us and to our children forever, that we may do all the words of this law.

Deuteronomy 29:29 NKJV

'But I, God, search the heart and examine the mind. I get to the heart of the human. I get to the root of things. I treat them as they really are, not as they pretend to be.'

Jeremiah 17:10 THE MESSAGE

Casting all your care upon Him, for He cares for you.

1 Peter 5:7 NKJV

Let the word of Christ richly dwell within you, with all wisdom teaching and admonishing one another with psalms and hymns and spiritual songs, singing with thankfulness in your hearts to God.

Colossians 3:16 NASB

Surely, I have taught you statutes and judgments, just as the LORD my God commanded me, that you should act according to them in the land which you go to possess. Therefore be careful to observe them; for this is your wisdom and your understanding in the sight of the peoples who will hear all these statutes, and say 'Surely this great nation is a wise and understanding people.'

Deuteronomy 4:5-6 NKJV

You shall love the LORD your God with all your heart, with all your soul, and with all your strength. And these words which I command you today shall be in your heart. You shall teach them diligently to your children, and shall talk of them when you sit in your house, when you walk by the way, when you lie down, and when you rise up.

Deuteronomy 6:5-7 NKJV

These things I have spoken to you, that you should not be made to stumble.

John 16:1 NKJV

Beware of false prophets, who come to you in sheep's clothing, but inwardly they are ravenous wolves. You will know them by their fruits. Do men gather grapes from thorn bushes or figs from thistles? Even so, every good tree bears good fruit, but a bad tree bears bad fruit. A good tree cannot bear bad fruit, nor can a bad tree bear good fruit...therefore by their fruits you will know them.

Matthew 7:15-18, 20 NKJV

The Lord was pleased that Solomon had asked for [Wisdom]. So God said to him, 'Since you have asked for this and not for long life or wealth for yourself, nor have asked for the death of your enemies but for discernment in administering justice, I will do what you have asked. I will give you a wise and discerning heart, so that there will never have been anyone like you, nor will there ever be. Moreover, I will give you what you have not asked for —both riches and honor—so that in your lifetime you will have no equal among kings. And if you walk in My ways and obey My statutes and commands as David your father did, I will give you a long life.'

1 Kings 3:10-14 NIV

Do not forget the covenant I have made with you, and do not worship or idolize other gods. Rather, worship the LORD your God. It is He who will deliver you from the hand of all your enemies.

2 Kings 17:38-39 NIV

The wise in heart are called prudent, understanding and knowing, and winsome speech increases learning in both speaker and listener. Understanding is a wellspring of life to those who have it, but to give instruction to fools is folly. The mind of the wise instructs his mouth, and adds learning and persuasiveness to his lips. Pleasant words are as a honeycomb, a sweet to the mind and healing to the body...he who is slow to anger is better than the mighty, he who rules his own spirit than he who takes a city.

Proverbs 16:21-24, 32 AMP

Jesus went on to make these comments: 'If you're honest in small things, you'll be honest in big things; If you're a crook in small things, you'll be a crook in big things. If you're not honest in small jobs, who will put you in charge of the store? No worker can serve two bosses: He'll either hate the first and love the second, or adore the first and despise the second. You can't serve both God and the Bank.'

Luke 16:13 THE MESSAGE

Therefore we do not lose heart. Even though outwardly we are wasting away, yet inwardly we are being renewed day by day. For our light and momentary troubles are achieving for us an eternal glory that far outweighs them all. So we fix our eyes not on what is seen, but on what is unseen. For what is seen is temporary, but what is unseen is eternal.

2 Corinthians 4:16-18 NIV

And this I pray, that your love may abound still more and more in knowledge and all discernment.

Philippians 1:9 NKJV

There is no way that God will reject a good person, and there is no way He'll help a bad one. God will let you laugh again. You'll raise the roof with shouts of joy, with your enemies thoroughly discredited, their house of cards collapsed.

Job 8:19-22 THE MESSAGE

We, of course, have plenty of wisdom to pass on to you once you get your feet on firm spiritual ground, but it's not popular wisdom, the fashionable wisdom of high-priced experts that will be out-of-date in a year or so. God's wisdom is something mysterious that goes deep into the interior of His purposes. You don't find it lying around on the surface. It's not the latest message, but more like the oldest - what God determined as the way to bring out His best in us, long before we ever arrived on the scene. The experts of our day haven't a clue about what this eternal plan is. If they had, they wouldn't have killed the Master of the God-designed life on a cross. That's why we have this Scripture text: No one's ever seen or heard anything like this. Never so much as imagined anything quite like it - What God has arranged for those who love Him. But you've seen and heard it because God by His Spirit has brought it all out into the open before you.

1 Corinthians 2:6-10 THE MESSAGE

Do you want to be counted wise, to build a reputation for wisdom? Here's what you do: Live well, live wisely, live humbly. It's the way you live, not the way you talk, that counts. Mean- spirited ambition isn't wisdom. Boasting that you are wise isn't wisdom. Twisting the truth to make yourselves sound wise isn't wisdom. It's the furthest thing from wisdom - it's animal cunning, devilish conniving. Whenever you're trying to look better than others or get the better of others, things fall apart and everyone ends up at the others' throats. Real wisdom, God's wisdom, begins with a holy life and is characterized by getting along with others. It is gentle and reasonable, overflowing with mercy and blessings, not hot one day and cold the next, not two-faced. You can develop a healthy, robust community that lives right with God and enjoy its results only if you do the hard work of getting along with each other, treating each other with dignity and honor.

James 3:13-18 THE MESSAGE

Many are the afflictions of the righteous, but the LORD delivers him out of them all.

Psalm 34:19 NKJV

And I have filled him with the Spirit of God, in wisdom, in understanding, in knowledge, and in all manner of workmanship.

Exodus 31:3 NKJV

Cast our burden on the LORD, and He shall sustain you; He shall never permit the righteous to be moved.

Psalm 55:22 NKJV

Who is wise and understanding among you? Let him show it by his good life, by deeds done in the humility (humbleness) that comes from wisdom. But if you harbor bitter envy and selfish ambition in your hearts, do not boast about it or deny the truth. Such 'wisdom' does not come down from heaven but is earthly, unspiritual, of the devil. For where you have envy and selfish ambition, there you find disorder and every evil practice. But the wisdom that comes from heaven is first of all pure; then peace-loving, considerate, submissive, full of mercy and good fruit, impartial and sincere. Peacemakers who sow in peace raise a harvest of righteousness.

James 3:13-18 NIV

With the merciful, You will show Yourself merciful. With the blameless man, You will show Yourself blameless. With the pure, You will show Yourself pure. And with the devious, You will show Yourself shrewd. For You will save the humble people, but You will bring down haughty looks.

Psalm 18:25-27 NKJV

A troublemaker plants seeds of strife; gossip separates the best of friends.

Proverbs 16:28 NLT

Do not fret because of evildoers, nor be envious of the workers of iniquity for they shall soon be cut down like the grass and wither as the green herb. Trust in the LORD and do good; dwell in the land, and feed on His faithfulness. Delight yourself also in the LORD and He shall give you the desires of your heart.

Psalm 37:1-4 NKJV

And this is the condemnation, that the light has come into the world, and men loved darkness rather than light, because their deeds were evil.

John 3:19 NKJV

Listen carefully: Unless a grain of wheat is buried in the ground, dead to the world, it is never any more than a grain of wheat. But if it is buried, it sprouts and reproduces itself many times over. In the same way, anyone who holds on to life just as it is destroys that life. But if you let it go, reckless in your love, you'll have it forever, real and eternal.

John 12:24-25 THE MESSAGE

Love prospers when a fault is forgiven, but dwelling on it separates close friends.

Proverbs 17:9 NLT

And I will give you shepherds according to My heart, who will feed you with knowledge and understanding.

Jeremiah 3:15 NKJV

I do it to encourage them. Then as their hearts are joined together in love, they will be wonderfully blessed with complete understanding. And they will truly know Christ. Not only is He the key to God's mystery, but all wisdom and knowledge are hidden away in Him. I tell you these things to keep you from being fooled by fancy talk. Even though I am not with you, I keep thinking about you. I am glad to know that you are living as you should and that your faith in Christ is strong. You have accepted Christ Jesus as your Lord. Now keep on following Him.

Colossians 2:2-6 CEV

'Call to Me and I will answer you, and show you great and mighty things, which you do not know.'

Jeremiah 33:3 NKJV

Dear Friends, the Bible teaches us so much about knowledge, understanding, and wisdom, especially in the books of Proverbs and Ecclesiastes in the Old Testament. Please make time to read them. You will love each verse, be in awe of its laser accuracy and how it applies to your everyday life.

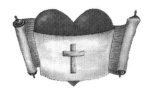

LOVE

To experience God's love and then to share it with others

For God so loved the world that He gave His only begotten Son, that whoever believes in Him should not perish but have everlasting life.

John 3:16 NKJV

Love God, your God, with your whole heart: love Him with all that's in you, love Him with all you've got!

Deuteronomy 6:5 THE MESSAGE

If you really fulfill the royal law according to the Scripture, 'you shall love your neighbor as yourself,' you do well.

James 2:8 NKJV

Let all that you do be done with love.

1 Corinthians 16:14 NKJV

Now that you've cleaned up your lives by following the Truth, love one another as if your lives depended on it. Your new life is not like your old life. Your old birth came from mortal sperm; your new birth comes from God's

126

living Word. Just think: a life conceived by God Himself! That's why the prophet said, 'The old life is a grass life, its beauty as short-lived as wildflowers; grass dries up, flowers droop, God's Word goes on and on forever. This is the Word that conceived the new life in you.'

1 Peter 1:22-25 THE MESSAGE

Finally, all of you be of one mind, having compassion for one another; love as brothers, be tender-hearted, be courteous.

1 Peter 3:8 NKJV

Then the Jews said, 'See how He loved him!'

John 11:36 NKJV

And then I'll marry you for good - forever! I'll marry you true and proper, in love and tenderness. Yes, I'll marry you and neither leave you nor let you go. You'll know me, God, for who I really am.'

Hosea 2:20 THE MESSAGE

Don't seek revenge or carry a grudge against any of your people. 'Love your neighbor as yourself.'

Leviticus 19:18 THE MESSAGE

If I could speak all the languages of earth and of angels, but didn't love others, I would only be a noisy gong or a clanging cymbal. If I had the gift of prophecy, and if I understood all of God's secret plans and possessed all knowledge, and if I had such faith that I could move mountains, but didn't love others, I would be nothing. If I gave everything I have to the poor and even sacrificed my body, I could boast about it; but if I didn't love others, I would have gained nothing. Love is patient and kind. Love is not jealous or boastful or proud or rude. It does not demand its own way. It is not irritable, and it keeps no record of being wronged. It does not rejoice about injustice but rejoices whenever the truth wins out. Love never gives up, never loses faith, is always hopeful, and endures through every circumstance. Prophecy and speaking in unknown languages and special knowledge will become useless. But love will last forever! Now our knowledge is partial and incomplete, and even the gift of prophecy reveals only part of the whole picture! But when full understanding comes, these partial things will become useless. When I was a child, I spoke and thought and reasoned as a child. But when I grew up, I put away childish things. We see things imperfectly as in a cloudy mirror, but then we will see everything with perfect clarity. All that I know now is partial and incomplete, but then I will know everything completely, just as God now knows me completely. Three things will last forever - faith, hope, and love - and the greatest of these is love.

1 Corinthians 13 NLT

Jesus said to him, 'You shall love the Lord your God with all your heart, with all your soul, and with all your mind...and the second is like it: You shall love your neighbor as yourself.'

Matthew 22:37, 39 NKJV

God passed in front of [Moses] and [he] called out, 'God, God, a God of mercy and grace, endlessly patient - so much love, so deeply true - loyal in love for a thousand generations, forgiving iniquity, rebellion, and sin.'

Exodus 34:4 THE MESSAGE

God, slow to get angry and huge in loyal love, forgiving iniquity and rebellion and sin; still, never just whitewashing sin.

Numbers 14:18 THE MESSAGE

Treat the foreigner the same as a native. Love him like one of your own. Remember that you were once foreigners in Egypt...

Leviticus 19:33 THE MESSAGE

And above all things have fervent love for one another, for 'love will cover a multitude of sins.' Be hospitable to one another without grumbling. As each one has received a gift, minister it to one another, as good stewards of the manifold grace of God.

1 Peter 4:8-10 NKJV

Make the Master proud of you by being good citizens. Respect the authorities, whatever their level; they are God's emissaries for keeping order. It is God's will that by doing good, you might cure the ignorance of the fools who think you're a danger to society. Exercise your freedom by serving God, not by breaking the rules. Treat everyone you meet with dignity. Love your spiritual family. Revere God. Respect the government.

1 Peter 2:13-17 THE MESSAGE

Love has been perfected among us in this: that we may have boldness in the day of judgment; because as He is, so are we in this world. There is no fear in love; but perfect love casts out fear, because fear involves torment. But he who fears has not been made perfect in love. We love Him because He first loved us.

1 John 4:17-19 NKJV

Entreat me not to leave you, or to turn back from following after you; for wherever you go, I will go; and wherever you lodge, I will lodge. Your people shall be my people, and your God my God. Where you die, I will die, and there will I be buried. The LORD do so to me, and more also, if anything but death parts you and me.

Ruth 1:16-17 NKJV

Let grace, mercy, and peace be with us in truth and love from God the Father and from Jesus Christ, Son of the Father!

2 John 1:3 THE MESSAGE

So husbands ought to love their own wives as their own bodies; he who loves his wife loves himself... Nevertheless let each one of you in particular so love his own wife as himself, and let the wife see that she respects her husband.

Ephesians 5:28, 33 NKJV

So, what do you think? With God on our side like this, how can we lose? If God didn't hesitate to put everything on the line for us, embracing our condition and exposing Himself to the worst by sending His own Son, is there anything else He wouldn't gladly and freely do for us? And who would dare tangle with God by messing with one of God's chosen? Who would dare even to point a finger? The One who died for us - who was raised to life for us - is in the presence of God at this very moment sticking up for us. Do you think anyone is going to be able to drive a wedge between us and Christ's love for us? There is no way! Not trouble, not hard times, not hatred, not hunger, not homelessness, not bullying threats, not backstabbing, not even the worst sins listed in Scripture: They kill us in cold blood because they hate you. We're sitting ducks; they pick us off one by one. None of this fazes us because Jesus loves us. I'm absolutely convinced that nothing - nothing living or dead, angelic or demonic, today or tomorrow, high or low, thinkable or unthinkable —absolutely nothing can get between us and God's love because of the way that Jesus our Master has embraced us.

Romans 8:31-39 THE MESSAGE

If anyone boasts, 'I love God,' and goes right on hating his brother or sister, thinking nothing of it, he is a liar. If he won't love the person he can see, how can he love the God he can't see? The command we have from Christ is blunt: Loving God includes loving people. You've got to love both.

1 John 4:20-21 THE MESSAGE

For the love of money [emphasis mine] is a root of all kinds of evil, for which some have strayed from the faith in their greediness, and pierced themselves through with many sorrows. But you, O man of God, flee these things and pursue righteousness, godliness, faith, love, patience, gentleness.

1 Timothy 6:10-11 NKJV

For this is the message that you heard from the beginning, that we should love one another... My little children, let us not love in word or in tongue, but in deed and in truth.

1 John 3:11, 18 NKJV

Beloved, let us love one another, for love is of God; and everyone who loves is born of God and knows God. He who does not love, does not know God, for God is love. In this the love of God was manifested toward us, that God has sent His only begotten Son into the world, that we might live through Him... Beloved, if God so loved us, we also ought to love one another... If we love one another, God abides in us, and His love has been perfected in us.

1 John 4:7-9, 11-12 NKJV

Mercy

When I need to be kinder, more compassionate and less judgmental

Praise the LORD of hosts, for the LORD is good, for His mercy endures forever!

Jeremiah 33:11 NKJV

Jonah was furious. He lost his temper. He yelled at God, 'God! I knew it - when I was back home, I knew this was going to happen! That's why I ran off to Tarshish! I knew you were sheer grace and mercy, not easily angered, rich in love, and ready at the drop of a hat to turn your plans of punishment into a program of forgiveness!'

Jonah 4:1-2 THE MESSAGE

Beloved, do not avenge yourselves...for it is written, 'vengeance is Mine, I will repay,' says the Lord.

Romans 12:19 NKJV

But He's already made it plain how to live, what to do, what God is looking for in men and women. It's quite simple: do what is fair and just to your neighbor, be compassionate and loyal in your love, and don't take yourself too seriously - take God seriously.

Micah 6:8 THE MESSAGE

You're familiar with the old written law, 'Love your friend,' and its unwritten companion, 'Hate your enemy.' I'm challenging that. I'm telling you to love your enemies. Let them bring out the best in you, not the worst. When someone gives you a hard time, respond with the energies of prayer, for then you are working out of your true selves, your God-created selves. This is what God does. He gives His best - the sun to warm and the rain to nourish - to everyone, regardless: the good and bad, the nice and nasty. If all you do is love the lovable, do you expect a bonus? Anybody can do that. If you simply say hello to those who greet you, do you expect a medal? Any run-of-the-mill sinner does that. In a word, what I'm saying is, grow up. You're kingdom subjects. Now live like it. Live out your God-created identity. Live generously and graciously toward others, the way God lives toward you.

Matthew 5:43-50 THE MESSAGE

A soft answer turns away wrath, but a harsh word stirs up anger.

Proverbs 15:1 NKJV

But to you who are willing to listen, I say, love your enemies! Do good to those who hate you. Bless those who curse you. Pray for those who hurt you. If someone slaps you on one cheek, offer the other cheek also. If someone demands your coat, offer your shirt also. Give to anyone who asks; and when things are taken away from you, don't try to get them back. Do to others as you would like them to do to you. If you love only those who love you, why should you get credit for that? Even sinners love those who love them! And if you do good only to those who do good to you, why should you get credit? Even sinners do that much! And if you lend money only to those who can repay you, why should you get credit? Even sinners will lend to other sinners for a full return. Love your enemies! Do good to them. Lend to them without expecting to be repaid. Then your reward from heaven will be very great, and you will truly be acting as children of the Most High, for He is kind to those who are unthankful and wicked. You must be compassionate, just as your Father is compassionate. Do not judge others, and you will not be judged. Do not condemn others, or it will all come back against you. Forgive others, and you will be forgiven. Give, and you will receive. Your gift will return to you in full - pressed down, shaken together to make room for more, running over, and poured into your lap. The amount you give will determine the amount you get back. Then Jesus gave the following illustration: 'Can one blind person lead another? Won't they both fall into a ditch?' Students are not greater than their teacher. But the student who is fully trained will become like the teacher. And why worry about a speck in your friend's eye when you have a log in your own? How can you think of saying, 'Friend, let me help you get rid of that speck in your eye,' when you can't see past the log in your own eye? Hypocrite! First get rid of the log in your own eye; then you will see well enough to deal with the speck in your friend's eye. 'This is My commandment, that you love one another as I have loved you. Greater love has no one than this, than to lay down one's life for his friends. You are My friends if you do whatever I command you. No longer do I call you servants, for a servant does not know what his master is doing. But I have called you friends for all things that I heard from My Father, I have made known to you.'

John 15:12-15 NLT

But I have trusted in Your mercy. My heart shall rejoice in Your salvation. I will sing to the LORD because He has dealt bountifully with me.

Psalm 13:5-6 NKJV

To the LORD our God belong mercy and forgiveness, though we have rebelled against Him.

Daniel 9:9 NKJV

So then, my beloved brethren, let every man be swift to hear, slow to speak, slow to wrath; for the wrath of man does not produce the righteousness of God.

James 1:19-20 NKJV

Remember me, O my God, concerning this also, and spare me according to the greatness of Your mercy!

Nehemiah 13:22 NKJV

But they, our ancestors, were arrogant; bull-headed, they wouldn't obey Your commands. They turned a deaf ear, they refuse to remember the miracles You had done for them; they turned stubborn, got it into their heads to return to their Egyptian slavery. And You, a forgiving God, gracious and compassionate, incredibly patient, with tons of love - You didn't dump them. Yes, even when they cast a sculpted calf and said, 'This is your god who brought you out of Egypt,' and continued from bad to worse, You in your amazing compassion didn't walk off and leave them in the desert. The Pillar of Cloud didn't leave them; daily it continued to show them their route; The Pillar of Fire did the same by night, showed them the right way to go. You gave them Your good Spirit to teach them to live wisely. You never stinted with Your manna, gave them plenty of water to drink. You supported them forty years in that desert; they had everything they needed; their clothes didn't wear out and their feet never blistered. You gave them kingdoms and peoples, establishing generous boundaries...You multiplied children for them, rivaling the stars in the night skies, and You brought them into the land that you promised their ancestors they would get and own. Well, they entered all right, they took it and settled in. The Canaanites who lived there, You brought to their knees before them. You turned over their land, kings, and peoples to do with as they pleased. They took strong cities and fertile fields, they took over well-furnished houses, cisterns, vineyards, olive groves, and lush, extensive orchards. And they ate, grew fat on the fat of the land; they reveled in Your bountiful goodness. But then they mutinied, rebelled against You, threw out Your laws and killed Your prophets, the very prophets who tried to get them back on Your side - and then things went from bad to worse. You turned them over to their enemies, who made life rough for them. But when they called out for help in their troubles, You listened from heaven; and in keeping with Your bottomless compassion, You gave them saviors: saviors who saved them from the cruel abuse of their enemies. But as soon as they had it easy again they were right back at it - even more evil. So You turned away and left them again to their fate, to the enemies who came right back. They cried out to You again; in your great compassion, You heard and helped them again. This went on over and over and over. You warned them to return to Your Revelation, they responded with haughty arrogance: They flouted Your commands, spurned your rules - the very words by which men and women live! They set their jaws in defiance, they turned their backs on You and didn't listen. You put up with them year after year and warned them by Your spirit through your prophets; but when they refused to listen You abandoned them to foreigners. Still, because of Your great compassion, You didn't make a total end to them. You didn't walk out and leave them for good; yes, You are a God of grace and compassion.

Nehemiah 9:16-31 THE MESSAGE

NURTURING

When I'm in need of God's tender arms of comfort

Blessed be the God and Father of our Lord Jesus Christ, the Father of mercies and God of all comfort, who comforts us in all our tribulation that we may be able to comfort those who are in any trouble, with the comfort with which we ourselves are comforted by God.

2 Corinthians 1:3-4 NKJV

Now may our Lord Jesus Christ Himself, and our God and Father, Who has loved us and given us everlasting consolation and good hope by grace, comfort your hearts and establish you in every good word and work.

2 Thessalonians 2:16-17 NKJV

And my God will meet all your needs according to His glorious riches in Christ Jesus.

Philippians 4:19 NIV

I will go before you and make the crooked places straight. I will break in pieces the gates of bronze and cut the bars of iron. I will give you the treasures of darkness and the hidden riches of secret places that you may know that I, the LORD, who call you by your name, AM, the God of Israel.

Isaiah 45:2-3 NKJV

I have called upon You, for You will hear me, O God. Incline Your ear to me, and hear my speech. Show Your marvelous loving kindness by Your right hand. O You, who save those who trust in You from those who rise up against them. Keep me as the apple of Your eye. Hide me under the shadow of Your wings from the wicked who oppress me from the deadly enemies who surround me... as for me, I will see Your face in righteousness. I shall be satisfied when I awake in Your likeness.

Psalm 17:6-9,15 NKJV

For we have great joy and consolation in your love because the hearts of the saints we have been refreshed by you, brother.

Philemon 1:7 NKJV

May the God of hope fill you with all joy and peace as you trust in Him, so that you may overflow with hope by the power of the Holy Spirit.

Romans 15:13 NIV

When you pass through the waters, I will be with you; and through the rivers, they shall not overflow you. When you walk through the fire, you shall not be burned, nor shall the flame scorch you.

Isaiah 43:2 NKJV

Show me Your ways, O LORD, teach me Your paths. Lead me in Your truth and teach me, for You are the God of my salvation. On You I wait all the day.

Psalm 25:4-5 NKJV

Lo, I am with you always, even to the end of the age.

Matthew 38:20 NKJV

...God, Who comforts and encourages and refreshes and cheers the depressed and the sinking...

2 Corinthians 7:6 AMP

But You are God, ready to pardon, gracious and merciful. Slow to anger, abundant in kindness, and You did not forsake us.

Nehemiah 9:17 NKJV

The LORD your God in your midst, the Mighty One, will save; He will rejoice over you with gladness, He will quiet you with His Love, He will rejoice over you with singing.

Zephaniah 3:17 NKJV

When my father and my mother forsake me, then the LORD will take care of me.

Psalm 27:10 NKJV

But immediately Jesus spoke to them saying, 'Be of good cheer! It is I; do not be afraid.'

Matthew 14:27 NKJV

Many sorrows come to the wicked, but unfailing love surrounds those who trust the LORD. So rejoice in the LORD and be glad, all you who obey Him! Shout for joy, all you whose hearts are pure!

Psalm 32:10-11 NLT

The LORD is near to those who have a broken heart, and saves such as have a contrite spirit.

Psalm 34:18 NKJV

Wait on the LORD; be of good courage, and He shall strengthen your heart; wait, I say, on the LORD!

Psalm 27:14 NKJV

For He Himself has said, 'I will never leave you nor forsake you.' So we may boldly say: 'The LORD is my helper; I will not fear. What can man do to me?'

Hebrews 13:5-6 NKJV

OBEDIENCE

When I am tempted into wrongdoing or insist on my own way

For this is the love of God, that we keep His commandments. And His commandments are not burdensome.

1 John 5:3 NKJV

My yoke is easy and My burden is light.

Matthew 11:30 NKJV

Don't sin by letting anger control you. Think about it overnight and remain silent. Offer sacrifices in the right spirit, and trust the LORD.

Psalm 4:4-5 NLT

Blessed are those who hear the Word of God and keep it.

Luke 11:28 NKJV

I now realize how true it is that God does not show favoritism, but accepts men from every nation who have reverence for Him and do what is right.

Acts 10:34-35 NIV

So here's what I want you to do, God helping you: Take your everyday, ordinary life - your sleeping, eating, going-to-work, and walking-around life - and place it before God as an offering. Embracing what God does for you is the best thing you can do for Him. Don't become so well-adjusted to your culture that you fit into it without even thinking. Instead, fix your attention on God. You'll be changed from the inside out. Readily recognize what He wants from you, and quickly respond to it. Unlike the culture around you, always dragging you down to its level of immaturity, God brings the best out of you, develops well-formed maturity in you.

Romans 12:1-2 THE MESSAGE

Listen, my son and be wise, and keep your heart on the right path. Do not join who drinks too much wine or gorge themselves on meat, for drunkards and gluttons become poor, and drowsiness clothes them in rages.

Proverbs 23:19-21 NIV

Behold, the maidservant of the Lord! Let it be to me according to Your Word.

Luke 1:38 NKJV

I tell you, love your enemies. Help and give without expecting a return. You'll never - I promise - regret it. Live out this God-created identity the way our Father lives toward us, generously and graciously, even when we're at our worst. Our Father is kind; you be kind.

Luke 6:35 NKJV

That's exactly what Jesus did. He didn't make it easy for Himself by avoiding people's troubles, but waded right in and helped out. 'I took on the troubles of the troubled,' is the way Scripture puts it. Even if it was written in Scripture long ago, you can be sure it's written for us. God wants the combination of His steady, constant calling and warm, personal counsel in Scripture to come to characterize us, keeping us alert for whatever He will do next. May our dependably steady and warmly personal God develop maturity in you so that you get along with each other as well as Jesus gets along with us all. Then we'll be a choir - not our voices only, but our very lives singing in harmony in a stunning anthem to the God and Father of our Master Jesus!

Romans 15:3-6 THE MESSAGE

A refusal to correct is a refusal to love; love your children by disciplining them.

Proverbs 13:24 THE MESSAGE

I can do all things through Christ Who strengthens me.

Philippians 4:13 NKJV

Blessed is the man who endures temptation; for when he has been approved, he will receive the crown of life which the Lord has promised to those who love Him.

James 1:12 NKJV

For He who would love life and see good days, let him refrain his tongue from evil, and his lips from speaking deceit.

1 Peter 3:10 NKJV

Trust God from the bottom of your heart; don't try to figure out everything on your own. Listen for God's voice in everything you do, everywhere you go; He's the one who will keep you on track. Don't assume that you know it all. Run to God! Run from evil! Your body will glow with health, your very bones will vibrate with life! Honor God with everything you own; give Him the first and the best. Your barns will burst, your wine vats will brim over. But don't, dear friend, resent God's discipline; don't sulk under His loving correction. It's the child He loves that God corrects; a father's delight is behind all this.

Proverbs 3:5-12 THE MESSAGE

Now therefore, if you will indeed obey My voice and keep My covenant, then you shall be a special treasure to Me above all people; for all the earth is Mine.

Exodus 19:5 NKJV

As you therefore have received Christ Jesus the Lord, so walk in Him.

Colossians 2:6 NKJV

Now get yourselves ready. I'm sending my Angel ahead of you to guard you in your travels, to lead you to the place that I've prepared. Pay close attention to him. Obey him. Don't go against him. He won't put up with your rebellions because he's acting on My authority. But if you obey him and do everything I tell you, I'll be an enemy to your enemies, I'll fight those who fight you...

Exodus 23:20-22 THE MESSAGE

But this is what I commanded them, saying, 'Obey My voice, and I will be your God, and you shall be My people. And walk in all the ways that I have commanded you, that it may be well with you.' Yet they did not obey or incline their ear, but followed the counsels and the dictates of their evil hearts, and went backward and not forward.

Jeremiah 7:23-24 NKJV

Whether it is pleasing or displeasing, we will obey the voice of the LORD our God to whom we send you, that it may be well with us when we obey the voice of the LORD our God.

Jeremiah 42:6 NKJV

So if you faithfully obey the commands I am giving you today - to love the LORD your God and to serve Him with all your heart and with all your soul - then I will send rain on your land in its season, both autumn and spring rains, so that you may gather in your grain, new wine and oil. I will provide grass in the fields for your cattle, and you will eat and be satisfied. Be careful, or you will be enticed to turn away and worship other gods and bow down to them. Then the LORD's anger will burn against you, and He will shut the heavens so that it will not rain and the ground will yield no produce, and you will soon perish from the good land the LORD is giving you. Fix these words of Mine in your hearts and minds; tie them as symbols on your hands and bind them on your foreheads. Teach them to your children, talking about them when you sit at home and when you walk along the road, when you lie down and when you get up. Write them on the doorframes of your houses and on your gates, so that your days and the days of your children may be many in the land that the LORD swore to give your forefathers, as many as the days that the heavens are above the earth. If you carefully observe all these commands I am giving you to follow - to love the LORD your God, to walk in all His ways and to hold fast to Him - then the LORD will drive out all these nations before you, and you will dispossess nations larger and stronger than you. Every place where you set your foot will be yours: Your territory will extend from the desert to Lebanon, and from the Euphrates River to the western sea. No man will be able to stand against you. The LORD your God, as He promised you, will put the terror and fear of you on the whole land, wherever you go.

Deuteronomy 11:13-25 NIV

And the people said to Joshua, 'the LORD our God we will serve, and His voice we will obey!'

Joshua 24:24 NKJV

Then Samuel said, 'Do you think all God wants are sacrifices - empty rituals just for show? He wants you to listen to [trust] Him! Plain listening is the thing, not staging a lavish religious production. Not doing what God tells you is far worse than fooling around in the occult. Getting self-important around God is far worse than making deals with your dead ancestors. Because [if] you [say] no to God's command, He [will] say no to your kingship.'

1 Samuel 15:22-23 THE MESSAGE

Then they were all amazed, so that they questioned among themselves, saying, 'What is this? What new doctrine is this? For with authority He commands even the unclean spirits, and they obey Him.'

Mark 1:27 NKJV

So the Lord said, 'If you have faith as a mustard seed, you can say to this mulberry tree, be pulled up by the roots and be planted in the sea, and it would obey you.'

Luke 17:6 NKJV

Peter and the other apostles replied, 'We must obey God rather than men!'

Acts 5:29 NIV

Remind the people to be subject to rulers and authorities, to be obedient, to be ready to do whatever is good, to slander no one, to be peaceable and considerate, and to show true humility toward all men. At one time we too were foolish, disobedient, deceived and enslaved by all kinds of passions and pleasures. We lived in malice and envy, being hated and hating one another. But when the kindness and love of God our Savior appeared, He saved us, not because of righteous things we had done, but because of His mercy. He saved us through the washing of rebirth and renewal by the Holy Spirit, whom He poured

*out on us generously through Jesus Christ our Savior, so
that, having been justified by His grace, we might become
heirs having the hope of eternal life. This is a trustworthy
saying. And I want you to stress these things, so that
those who have trusted in God may be careful to devote
themselves to doing what is good. These things are
excellent and profitable for everyone. But avoid foolish
controversies and genealogies and arguments and
quarrels about the law, because these are unprofitable
and useless. Warn a divisive person once, and then warn
him a second time. After that, have nothing to do with
him.*

Titus 3:1-10 NIV

*But for those who are self-seeking and who reject the
truth and follow evil, there will be wrath and anger.
There will be trouble and distress for every human being
who does evil: first for the Jew, then for the Gentile; but
glory, honor and peace for everyone who does good...For
God does not show favoritism.*

Romans 2:8-11 NIV

*Children, obey your parents in all things, for this is well
pleasing to the Lord.*

Colossians 3:20 NKJV

*Summing up: Be agreeable, be sympathetic, be loving, be
compassionate, be humble. That goes for all of you, no
exceptions. No retaliation. No sharp- tongued sarcasm.
Instead, bless - that's your job, to bless. You'll be a
blessing and also get a blessing. Whoever wants to
embrace life and see the day fill up with good, here's
what you do: say nothing evil or hurtful; snub evil and
cultivate good; run after peace for all you're worth. God
looks on all this with approval, listening and responding
well to what He's asked; but He turns His back on those
who do evil things. If with heart and soul you're doing*

good, do you think you can be stopped? Even if you suffer for it, you're still better off. Don't give the opposition a second thought. Through thick and thin, keep your hearts at attention, in adoration before Christ, your Master. Be ready to speak up and tell anyone who asks why you're living the way you are, and always with the utmost courtesy. Keep a clear conscience before God so that when people throw mud at you, none of it will stick. They'll end up realizing that they're the ones who need a bath. It's better to suffer for doing good, if that's what God wants, than to be punished for doing bad. That's what Christ did definitively; suffered because of others' sins, the Righteous One for the unrighteous ones. He went through it all - was put to death and then made alive to bring us to God.

1 Peter 3:8-18 THE MESSAGE

Since you have purified your souls in obeying the truth through the Spirit in sincere love of the brethren, love one another fervently with a pure heart.

1 Peter 1:22 NKJV

When we put bits into the mouths of horses to make them obey us, we can turn the whole animal. Or take ships as an example. Although they are so large and are driven by strong winds, they are steered by a very small rudder wherever the pilot wants to go. Likewise the tongue is a small part of the body, but it makes great boasts. Consider what a great forest is set on fire by a small spark. The tongue also is a fire, a world of evil among the parts of the body. It corrupts the whole person, sets the whole course of his life on fire, and is itself set on fire by hell. All kinds of animals, birds, reptiles and creatures of the sea are being tamed and have been tamed by man, but no man can tame the tongue. It is a restless evil, full of deadly poison. With the tongue we praise our Lord and Father, and with it we curse men, who have been made in

God's likeness. Out of the same mouth come praise and cursing. My brothers, this should not be. Can both fresh water and salt water flow from the same spring? My brothers, can a fig tree bear olives, or a grapevine bear figs? Neither can a salt spring produce fresh water.

James 3:3-12 NIV

See that you walk circumspectly, not as fools but as wise...

Ephesians 5:15 NKJV

That means you must not give sin a vote in the way you conduct your lives. Don't give it the time of day. Don't even run little errands that are connected with that old way of life. Throw yourselves wholeheartedly and full-time - remember, you've been raised from the dead - into God's way of doing things. Sin can't tell you how to live. After all, you're not living under that old tyranny any longer. You're living in the freedom of God.

Romans 6:12-14 THE MESSAGE

Watch and pray, lest you enter into temptation. The spirit indeed is willing, but the flesh is weak.

Matthew 26:41 NKJV

What I'm getting at, friends, is that you should simply keep on doing what you've done from the beginning. When I was living among you, you lived in responsive obedience. Now that I'm separated from you, keep it up. Better yet, redouble your efforts. Be energetic in your life of salvation, reverent and sensitive before God. That energy is God's energy, an energy deep within you, God Himself willing... Do everything readily and cheerfully - no bickering, no second-guessing allowed! Go out into the world uncorrupted, a breath of fresh air in this squalid and polluted society. Provide people with a glimpse of good living and of the living God. Carry the

Light-giving Message into the night so I'll have good cause to be proud of you on the day that Christ returns.

Philippians 2:12-16 THE MESSAGE

Observe and obey all these words which I command you, that it may go well with you and your children after you forever, when you do what is good and right in the sight of the LORD your God.

Deuteronomy 12:28 NKJV

For though we live in the world, we do not wage war as the world does. The weapons we fight with are not the weapons of the world. On the contrary, they have divine power to demolish strongholds. We demolish arguments and every pretension that sets itself up against the knowledge of God, and we take captive every thought to make it obedient to Christ.

2 Corinthians 10:3-5 NIV

PEACE

When I need assurance in the midst of uncertainties

Be anxious for nothing, but in everything by prayer and supplication with thanksgiving let your requests be made known to God. And the peace of God, which surpasses all comprehension will guard your hearts and your minds in Christ Jesus.

Philippians 4:6-7 NASB

The LORD bless you and keep you. The LORD make His face shine upon you, and be gracious to you; the LORD lift up His countenance upon you, and give you peace.

Numbers 6:24-26 NKJV

And the effect of righteousness will be peace, internal and external, and the result of righteousness will be quietness, and confident trust forever.

Isaiah 32:17 AMP

Peace I leave with you. My peace I give to you; not as the world gives, but as I give to you. Let not your heart be troubled, neither let it be afraid.

John 14:27 NKJV

Let the peace of God rule in your hearts.

Colossians 3:15 NKJV

You will keep him in perfect peace, whose mind is stayed on You, because he trusts in You. Trust in the LORD forever for the LORD is everlasting strength.

Isaiah 26:3-4 NKJV

The Spirit Himself bears witness with our spirit that we are children of God, and if children, then heirs – heirs of God and joint heirs with Christ, if indeed we suffer with Him, that we may also be glorified together.

Romans 8:16-17 NKJV

These things I have spoken to you, that in Me you may have peace. In the world you will have tribulation; but be of good cheer, I have overcome the world.

John 16:33 NKJV

As the Father loved Me, I also have loved you; abide in My love.

John 15:9 NKJV

The one who sows to please his sinful nature, from that nature will reap destruction; the one who sows to please the Spirit, from the Spirit will reap eternal life. Let us not become weary in doing good, for at the proper time we will reap a harvest if we do not give up. Therefore, as we have opportunity, let us do good to all people, especially to those who belong to the family of believers.

Galatians 6:8-10 NIV

Cast your burden on the LORD, and He shall sustain you; He shall never permit the righteous to be moved.

Psalm 55:22 NKJV

Now may the Lord direct your hearts into the love of God and into the patience of Christ.

2 Thessalonians 3:5 NKJV

Therefore, having been justified by faith, we have peace with God through our Lord Jesus Christ, through whom also we have obtained our introduction by faith into this grace in which we stand; and we exult in hope of the glory of God. And not only this, but we also exult in our tribulations, knowing that tribulation brings about perseverance; and perseverance proven character; and proven character, hope; and hope does not disappoint, because the love of God has been poured out within our hearts through the Holy Spirit who was given to us, for while we were still helpless, at the right time, Christ died for the ungodly.

Romans 5:1-6 NASB

Why are you cast down, O my soul? And why are you disquieted within me? Hope in God; for I shall yet praise Him, the help of my countenance and my God.

Psalm 43:5 NKJV

This is My commandment, that you love one another as I have loved you. Greater love has no one than this, than to lay down one's life for his friends.

John 15: 12-13 NKJV

I waited patiently for the LORD and He inclined to me, and He heard my cry. He also brought me up out of a horrible pit, out of the miry clay and set my feet upon a rock and established my steps. He has put a new song in my mouth – praise to our God; many will see it and fear and will trust in the LORD.

Psalm 40:1-3 NKJV

Now if God clothes the grass of the filed, which today is, and tomorrow is thrown into the oven, will He not much more clothe you...?

Matthew 6:30 NKJV

Grace, mercy and peace from God the Father and Christ Jesus our Lord.

1 Timothy 1:2 NIV

And my God shall supply all your needs according to His riches in glory by Christ Jesus.

Philippians 4:19 NKJV

Be at peace among yourselves.

1 Thessalonians 5:13 NKJV

Each one of you is part of the body of Christ, and you were chosen to live together in peace. So let the peace that comes from Christ control your thoughts. And be grateful.

Colossians 3:15 CEV

Cast all your care upon Him, for He cares for you.

1 Peter 5:7 NKJV

The grace of our Lord was poured out on me abundantly, along with the faith and love that are in Christ Jesus.

1 Timothy 1:14 NIV

Peace to the brethren, and love with faith, from God the Father and the Lord Jesus Christ. Grace be with all those who love our Lord Jesus Christ in sincerity. Amen.

Ephesians 6:23-24 NKJV

For this child I prayed, and the LORD has granted me my petition which I asked of Him.

1 Samuel 1:27 NKJV

The LORD is my shepherd; I shall not want. He makes me to lie down in green pastures; He leads me beside the still waters. He restores my soul; He leads me in the paths of righteousness for His name's sake. Yea, though I walk through the valley of the shadow of death, I will fear no evil; for You are with me; Your rod and Your staff, they comfort me. You prepare a table before me in the presence of my enemies; You anoint my head with oil; my cup runs over. Surely goodness and mercy shall follow me all the days of my life; and I will dwell in the house of the LORD forever.

Psalm 23 NKJV

And thus you shall say to him who lives in prosperity: 'peace be to you, peace to your house, and peace to all that you have!'

1 Samuel 25:6 NKJV

All your children shall be taught by the LORD, and great shall be the peace of your children.

Isaiah 54:13 NKJV

Perseverance

When I am stretched, overwhelmed, and feel like giving up

Blessed is the man who perseveres under trial, because when he has stood the test, he will receive the crown of life that God has promised to those who love Him.

James 1:12 NIV

Being confident of this very thing, that He who has began a good work in you will complete it until the day of Jesus Christ.

Philippians 1:6 NKJV

Not only so, but we also rejoice in our sufferings, because we know that suffering produces perseverance; perseverance, character; and character, hope. And hope does not disappoint us, because God has poured out His love into our hearts by the Holy Spirit, whom He has given us.

Romans 5:3-5 NIV

Whatever things you ask in prayer, believing, you will receive.

Matthew 21:22 NKJV

No man shall be able to stand before you all the days of your life. As I was with Moses, so I will be with you. I will not leave you nor forsake you. Be strong and of good courage...only be strong and very courageous, that you may observe to do according to all the law which Moses, My servant commanded you. Do not turn from it to the right hand or to the left, that you may prosper wherever you go. This Book of the Law shall not depart from your mouth, but you shall meditate in it day and night, that you may observe to do according to all that is written in it. For then you will make your way prosperous, and then you will have good success. Have I commanded you? Be strong and of good courage; do not be afraid, nor be dismayed, for the LORD your God is with you wherever you go.

Joshua 1:5-9 NKJV

Work your garden - you'll end up with plenty of food; play and party - you'll end up with an empty plate. Committed and persistent work pays off; get- rich- quick schemes are rip-offs. Playing favorites is always a bad thing; you can do great harm in seemingly harmless ways.

Proverbs 28:19-21 THE MESSAGE

No temptation has overtaken you except such as is common to man; but God is faithful, who will not allow you to be tempted beyond what you are able, but with the temptation will also make the way of escape, that you may be able to bear it.

1 Corinthians 10:13 NKJV

When I asked for Your help, You answered my prayer and gave me courage.

Psalm 138:3 CEV

You guide me with Your counsel, and afterward You will take me into glory.

Psalm 73:24 NIV

I say then; walk in the spirit, and you shall not fulfill the lust of the flesh.

Galatians 5:16 NKJV

We are hard-pressed on every side, yet not crushed; we are perplexed, but not in despair, persecuted, but not forsaken; struck down but not destroyed.

2 Corinthians 4:8-9 NKJV

Watch and pray, lest you enter into temptation. The spirit indeed is willing, but the flesh is weak.

Matthew 26:41 NKJV

For God did not appoint us to wrath, but to obtain salvation through our Lord Jesus Christ, who died for us, that whether we wake or sleep, we should live together with Him. Therefore, comfort each other and edify one another just as you also are doing.

1 Thessalonians 5:9-11 NKJV

A final word: Be strong in the Lord and in His mighty power. Put on all of God's armor so that you will be able to stand firm against all the strategies of the devil. For we are not fighting against flesh and blood enemies, but against evil rulers and authorities of the unseen world, against mighty powers in this dark world, and against evil spirits in the heavenly places. Therefore, put on every piece of God's armor so you will be able to resist the enemy in the time of evil. Then after the battle, you will be standing firm. Stand your ground, putting on the belt of truth and the body armor of God's righteousness. For shoes, put on the peace that comes from the Good News so that you will be fully prepared. In addition to all of these, hold up the shield of faith to stop the fiery arrows of the devil. Put on salvation as your helmet, and take the sword of the Spirit, which is the Word of God. Pray in the Spirit at all times and on every occasion. Stay alert and be persistent in your prayers for all believers everywhere.

Ephesians 6:10-18 NLT

...Forgetting what is behind and straining toward what is ahead, I press on toward the goal to win the prize for which God has called me heavenward in Christ Jesus.

Philippians 3:13-14 NIV

But you, my dear friends, must remember what the apostles of our Lord Jesus Christ said. They told you that in the last times there would be scoffers whose purpose in life is to satisfy their ungodly desires. These people are the ones who are creating divisions among you. They follow their natural instincts because they do not have God's Spirit in them. But you, dear friends, must build each other up in your most holy faith, pray in the power of the Holy Spirit, and await the mercy of our Lord Jesus Christ, who will bring you eternal life. In this way, you will keep yourselves safe in God's love. And you must show mercy to those whose faith is wavering. Rescue others by snatching them from the flames of judgment. Show mercy to still others, but do so with great caution, hating the sins that contaminate their lives. Now all glory to God, who is able to keep you from falling away and will bring you with great joy into His glorious presence without a single fault. All glory to Him who alone is God, our Savior through Jesus Christ our Lord. All glory, majesty, power, and authority are His before all time, and in the present, and beyond all time! Amen.

Jude 1:17-25 NLT

Every time we think of you, we thank God for you. Day and night you're in our prayers as we call to mind your work of faith, your labor of love, and your patience of hope in following our Master, Jesus Christ, before God our Father. It is clear to us, friends, that God not only loves you very much but also has put His hand on you for something special. When the Message we preached came to you, it wasn't just words. Something happened in you. The Holy Spirit put steel in your convictions.

1 Thessalonians 1:2-5 THE MESSAGE

PURPOSE

To know that God has uniquely created me for a special calling

Most assuredly, I say to you, he who believes in Me, the works that I do, he will do also; and greater works than these he will do because I go to My Father and whatever you ask in My Name, that I will do, that the Father may be glorified in the Son. If you ask anything in My Name, I will do it.

John 14:12-14 NKJV

We have different gifts according, to the grace given us.

Romans 12:6 NIV

For you, brethren, have been called to liberty; only do not use liberty as an opportunity for the flesh, but through love serve one another. For all the law is fulfilled in one word, even in this: 'you shall love your neighbor as yourself.'

Galatians 5:13-14 NKJV

The Spirit of the LORD God is upon Me, for the LORD has anointed Me to bring good news to the poor. He has sent Me to comfort the broken-hearted and to proclaim that captives will be released and prisoners will be freed. He has sent Me to tell those who mourn that the time of the LORD's favor has come, and with it, the day of God's anger against their enemies. To all who mourn in Israel, He will give a crown of beauty for ashes, a joyous blessing instead of mourning, festive praise instead of despair. In their righteousness, they will be like great oaks that the LORD has planted for His own glory.

Isaiah 61:1-3 NLT

Walking along the beach of Lake Galilee, Jesus saw two brothers: Simon (later called Peter) and Andrew. They were fishing, throwing their nets into the lake. It was their regular work. Jesus said to them, 'Come with me. I'll make a new kind of fisherman out of you. I'll show you how to catch men and women instead of perch and bass.' They didn't ask questions, but simply dropped their nets and followed.

Matthew 4:18-20 NKJV

We make it our aim to be well pleasing to our Lord Jesus Christ.

2 Corinthians 5:9 NKJV

Sanctify yourselves, for tomorrow the LORD will do wonders among you.

Joshua 3:5 NKJV

Do not neglect the gift that is in you.

1 Timothy 4:14 NKJV

Because of this decision we don't evaluate people by what they have or how they look. We looked at the Messiah that way once and got it all wrong, as you know. We certainly don't look at Him that way anymore. Now we look inside, and what we see is that anyone united with the Messiah gets a fresh start, is created new. The old life is gone; a new life burgeons! Look at it! All this comes from the God who settled the relationship between us and Him, and then called us to settle our relationships with each other. God put the world square with Himself through the Messiah, giving the world a fresh start by offering forgiveness of sins. God has given us the task of telling everyone what He is doing. We're Christ's representatives. God uses us to persuade men and women to drop their differences and enter into God's work of making things right between them. We're speaking for Christ Himself now: Become friends with God; He's already a friend with you.

2 Corinthians 5:16-20 THE MESSAGE

Their purpose is to teach people wisdom and discipline, to help them understand the insights of the wise. Their purpose is to teach people to live disciplined and successful lives, to help them do what is right, just, and fair.

Proverbs 1:1-3 NLT

Therefore, as we have opportunity, let us do good to all, especially to those who are of the household of faith.

Galatians 6:10 NKJV

Yet who knows whether you have come to the kingdom for such a time as this?

Esther 4:14 NKJV

Jesus now called the Twelve and gave them authority and power to deal with all the demons and cure diseases. He commissioned them to preach the news of God's kingdom and heal the sick. He said, 'Don't load yourselves up with equipment. Keep it simple; you are the equipment. And no luxury inns — get a modest place and be content there until you leave. If you're not welcomed, leave town. Don't make a scene. Shrug your shoulders and move on.'

Luke 9:1-5 THE MESSAGE

Because we know that this extraordinary day is just ahead, we pray for you all the time - pray that our God will make you fit for what He's called you to be, pray that He'll fill your good ideas and acts of faith with His own energy so that it all amounts to something. If your life honors the Name of Jesus, He will honor you. Grace is behind and through all of this, our God giving Himself freely, the Master, Jesus Christ, giving Himself freely.

2 Thessalonians 1:11-12 THE MESSAGE

For this purpose I have raised you up that I may show My power in you and that My Name might be declared in all that be declared in all the earth.

Romans 9:17 NKJV

'For I know the plans I have for you,' says the LORD. 'They are plans for good and not for evil, to give you a future and a hope.'

Jeremiah 29:11 NKJV

But I have spared you for a purpose - to show you My power and to spread My Name throughout the earth.

Exodus 9:16 NLT

I cry out to the Most High, to God Who will fulfill His purpose for me.

Psalm 57:2 NLT

The thief's [devil's] purpose is to steal and kill and destroy. My purpose is to give [you] a rich and satisfying life.

John 10:10 NLT

I tell you the truth, until heaven and earth disappear, not even the smallest detail of God's law will disappear until its purpose is achieved.

Matthew 5:18 NLT

It is absolutely clear that God has called you to a free life. Just make sure that you don't use this freedom as an excuse to do whatever you want to do and destroy your freedom. Rather, use your freedom to serve one another in love; that's how freedom grows. For everything we know about God's Word is summed up in a single sentence: Love others as you love yourself. That's an act of true freedom. If you bite and ravage each other, watch out - in no time at all you will be annihilating each other, and where will your precious freedom be then? My counsel is this: Live freely, animated and motivated by God's Spirit. Then you won't feed the compulsions of selfishness. For there is a root of sinful self-interest in us that is at odds with a free spirit, just as the free spirit is incompatible with selfishness. These two ways of life are antithetical, so that you cannot live at times one way and at times another way according to how you feel on any given day. Why don't you choose to be led by the Spirit and so escape the erratic compulsions of a law-dominated existence? It is obvious what kind of life develops out of trying to get your own way all the time: repetitive, loveless, cheap sex; a stinking accumulation of mental and emotional garbage; frenzied and joyless grabs for happiness; trinket gods; magic-show religion; paranoid loneliness; cutthroat competition; all-consuming-yet-never-satisfied wants; a brutal temper; an impotence to love or be loved; divided homes and divided lives; small-minded and lopsided pursuits; the vicious habit of depersonalizing everyone into a rival; uncontrolled and uncontrollable addictions; ugly parodies of community. I could go on. This isn't the first time I have warned you, you know. If you use your freedom this way, you will not inherit God's kingdom. But what happens when we live God's way? He brings gifts into our lives, much the same way that fruit appears in an orchard - things like affection for others, exuberance about life, serenity. We develop a willingness to stick with things, a sense of compassion in the heart, and a conviction that a basic holiness permeates things and people. We find ourselves involved in loyal commitments, not needing to force our way in life, able to marshal and direct our energies wisely. Legalism is helpless in bringing this about; it only gets in the way. Among those who belong to Christ, everything connected with getting our own way and mindlessly responding to what everyone else calls necessities is killed off for good - crucified. Since this is the kind of life we have chosen, the life of the Spirit, let us make sure that we do not just hold it as an idea in our heads or a sentiment in our hearts, but work out its implications in every detail of our lives. That means we will not compare ourselves with each other as if one of us were better and another worse. We have far more interesting things to do with our lives. Each of us is an original.

Galatians 5:15-26 NLT

I will raise up Cyrus to fulfill my righteous purpose, and I will guide his actions. He will restore my city and free my captive people - without seeking a reward! I, the LORD of heaven's armies, have spoken!

Isaiah 45:13 NLT

The purpose of my instruction is that all believers would be filled with love that comes from a pure heart, a clear conscience, and genuine faith.

1 Timothy 1:5 NLT

You show that you are a letter from Christ, the result of our ministry, written not with ink but with the Spirit of the living God, not on tablets of stone, but on tablets of human hearts.

2 Corinthians 3:3 NIV

QUIETNESS

When I need uninterrupted time with God to hear His voice

Peace, I leave with you. My peace I give to you, not as the world gives do I give to you. Let not your heart be troubled, neither let it be afraid. You have heard Me say to you, I am going away and coming back to you.

John 14:27-28 NKJV

Here's what I want you to do: Find a quiet, secluded place so you won't be tempted to role-play before God. Just be there as simply and honestly as you can manage. The focus will shift from you to God, and you will begin to sense His grace.

Matthew 6:6 THE MESSAGE

Whether you turn to the right or to the left, your ears will hear a voice behind you, saying 'this is the way; walk in it'.

Isaiah 30:21 NIV

To you it was shown, that you might know that the LORD Himself is God; there is none other besides Him. Out of heaven He let you hear His voice, that He might instruct you.

Deuteronomy 4:35-36 NKJV

God, my shepherd! I don't need a thing. You have bedded me down in lush meadows, you find me quiet pools to drink from. True to Your word, You let me catch my breath and send me in the right direction.

Psalm 23:1 THE MESSAGE

I'm asking God for one thing, only one thing: to live with Him in His house my whole life long. I'll contemplate His beauty; I'll study at His feet. That's the only quiet, secure place in a noisy world, the perfect getaway, far from the buzz of traffic. God holds me head and shoulders above all who try to pull me down. I'm headed for His place to offer anthems that will raise the roof! Already I'm singing God-songs; I'm making music to God.

Psalm 27:4-6 THE MESSAGE

Quiet. Listen obediently...this very day you have become the people of God, your God. Listen to the voice of your God.

Deuteronomy 27:9 THE MESSAGE

A quietly given gift soothes an irritable person; a heartfelt present cools a hot temper.

Proverbs 21:14 THE MESSAGE

Because of the LORD's great love, we are not consumed, for His compassions never fail. They are new every morning; great is Your faithfulness.

Lamentations 3:22-23 NIV

When you knock on a door, be courteous in your greeting. If they welcome you, be gentle in your conversation. If they don't welcome you, quietly withdraw. Don't make a scene. Shrug your shoulders and be on your way.

Matthew 10:12 THE MESSAGE

As the Father loved Me, I also have loved you; abide in My love. If you keep My commandments, you will abide in My love, just as I have kept My Father's commandments and abide in His love. These things I have spoken to you, that My joy may remain in you and that your joy may be full.

John 15:9-11 NKJV

Better is a dry morsel with quietness than a house full of feasting with strife.

Proverbs 17:1 NKJV

In the same way, the Spirit helps us in our weakness. We do not know what we ought to pray for, but the Spirit Himself intercedes for us through wordless groans. And He who searches our hearts knows the mind of the Spirit, because the Spirit intercedes for God's people in accordance with the will of God.

Romans 8:26-27 THE MESSAGE

Mean-spirited slander is heartless; quiet discretion accompanies good sense.

Proverbs 11:12 THE MESSAGE

Open up before GOD, keep nothing back; He'll do whatever needs to be done: He'll validate your life in the clear light of day and stamp you with approval at high noon. Quiet down before GOD, be prayerful before Him.

Psalm 37:5-8 THE MESSAGE

Let your light so shine before men, that they may see your good works and glorify your Father in heaven.

Matthew 5:16 NKJV

You're my place of quiet retreat; I wait for Your Word to renew me.

Psalm 119:113 THE MESSAGE

My soul, wait silently for God alone. For my expectation is from Him. He only is my rock and my salvation. He is my defense; I shall not be moved.

Psalm 62:5-6 NKJV

The quiet words of the wise are more effective than the ranting of a king of fools.

Ecclesiastes 9:17 THE MESSAGE

And whenever you stand praying, if you have anything against anyone, forgive him, that your Father in heaven may also forgive you, your trespasses.

Mark 11:25 NKJV

Whatever things you ask in prayer, believing, you will receive.

Matthew 21:22 NKJV

If any of you lacks wisdom, he should ask God, who gives generously to all without finding fault, and it will be given to him. But when he asks, he must believe and not doubt, because he who doubts is like a wave of the sea, blown and tossed by the wind. That man should not think he will receive anything from the Lord; he is a double-minded man, unstable in all he does.

James 1:5-8 NIV

I will pray with the Spirit, and I will also pray with the understanding. I will sing with the Spirit, and I will also sing with the understanding.

1 Corinthians 14:15 NKJV

Are you tired? Worn out? Burned out on religion? Come to Me. Get away with Me and you'll recover your life. I'll show you how to take a real rest. Walk with Me and work with Me - watch how I do it. Learn the unforced rhythms of grace. I won't lay anything heavy or ill-fitting on you. Keep company with Me and you'll learn to live freely and lightly.

Matthew 11:28-30 THE MESSAGE

God proves to be good to the man who passionately waits, to the woman who diligently seeks. It's a good thing to quietly hope, quietly hope for help from God. It's a good thing when you're young to stick it out through the hard times. So too, the Holy Spirit comes to our aid and bears us up in our weakness; for we do not know what prayer to offer nor how to offer it worthily as we ought, but the Spirit Himself goes to meet our supplication and pleads in our behalf with unspeakable yearnings and groanings too deep for utterance. And He Who searches the hearts of men knows what is in the mind of the Holy Spirit what His intent is, because the Spirit intercedes and pleads before God in behalf of the saints according to and in harmony with God's will.

Lamentations 3:24-26 THE MESSAGE

Therefore, confess your sins to one another, and pray for one another so that you may be healed. The effective prayer of a righteous man can accomplish much.

James 5:16 NASB

Your word I have hidden in my heart, that I might not sin against You.

Psalm 119:11 NKJV

And when they had prayed, the place where they were assembled together was shaken; and they were all filled with the Holy Spirit, and they spoke the Word of God with boldness.

Acts 4:31 NKJV

Grace to you and peace from God our Father and the Lord Jesus Christ. I thank my God, making mention of you always in my prayers, hearing of your love and faith which you have toward the Lord Jesus and toward all the saints, that the sharing of your faith may become effective by the acknowledgment of every good thing which is in you in Christ Jesus.

Philemon 1:3-6 NKJV

Rest

When I am weary

Come to Me, all you who labor and are heavy laden, and I will give you rest. Take My yoke upon you and learn from Me, for I am gentle and humble in heart, and you will find rest for your souls. For My yoke is easy and My burden is light.

Matthew 11:28-30 NKJV

Work six days and rest the seventh.

Exodus 34:21 THE MESSAGE

Blessed are all those who put their trust in Him.

Psalm 2:12 NKJV

This is the time and place to rest, to give rest to the weary. This is the place to lay down your burden.

Isaiah 28:11 THE MESSAGE

But so many people were coming and going that Jesus and the apostles did not even have a chance to eat. Then Jesus said, 'Let's go to a place where we can be alone and get some rest.'

Mark 6:31 THE MESSAGE

The LORD is giving you rest and is giving you this land.

Joshua 1:13 NKJV

There they rested and were revived.

2 Samuel 16:14 THE MESSAGE

What then shall we say to all this? If God is for us, who can be against us? Who can be our foe, if God is on our side? He who did not withhold or spare even His own Son, but gave Him up for us all, will He not also with Him, freely and graciously give us all other things?

Romans 8:31-32 AMP

I'll refresh tired bodies; I'll restore tired souls.

Jeremiah 31:25 THE MESSAGE

The Spirit of God gave them rest.

Isaiah 63:11 THE MESSAGE

'We have this peaceful land because we sought God; He has given us rest from all troubles.' So they built and enjoyed prosperity.

2 Chronicles 14: 7 THE MESSAGE

On that day God's people will rest from their work, just as God rested from His work. We should do our best to enter that place of rest, so that none of us will disobey and miss going there, as they did. What God has said isn't only alive and active! It is sharper than any double-edged sword. His word can cut through our spirits and souls and through our joints and marrow, until it discovers the desires and thoughts of our hearts.

Hebrews 4:10-12 THE MESSAGE

Rest in the LORD and wait patiently for Him. Do not fret because of him who prospers in his way, because of the man who brings wicked schemes to pass. Cease from anger and forsake wrath. Do not fret – it only causes harm. For evil doers shall be cut off, but those who wait on the LORD, they shall inherit the earth. For yet a little while, and the wicked shall be no more. But the meek shall inherit the earth, and shall delight themselves in the abundance of peace.

Psalm 37:7-11 NKJV

Sit down and rest, everyone.   Recover your strength. Gather around Me. Say what's on your heart. Together let's decide what's right.

Isaiah 41:1 THE MESSAGE

God's people must learn to endure. They must also obey His commands and have faith in Jesus. Then I heard a voice from heaven say, 'Put this in writing. From now on, the Lord will bless everyone who has faith in Him when they die.'   The Spirit answered, 'Yes, they will rest from their hard work, and they will be rewarded for what they have done.'

Revelation 14:12-14 THE MESSAGE

And I will pray to the Father and He will give you another Helper that He may abide with you forever.

John 14:16 NKJV

Blessed are all those who put their trust in Him.

Psalm 2:12 NKJV

Don't continue doing things the way we're doing them at present, each of us doing as we wish.   Until now you haven't arrived at the goal, the resting place, the inheritance that God, your God, is giving you.   But the minute you cross the Jordan River and settle into the land

God, your God, is enabling you to inherit, He'll give you rest from all your surrounding enemies. You'll be able to settle down and live in safety.

Deuteronomy 12:8 THE MESSAGE

Restoration

For God to renew me, and to return all the things the enemy has stolen from me

In His kindness God called you to share in His eternal glory by means of Christ Jesus. So after you have suffered a little while, He will restore, support, and strengthen you, and He will place you on a firm foundation. All power to Him forever! Amen.

1 Peter 5:10-11 NLT

'I'll restore everything that was lost in this land. I'll make everything as good as new. I, God, say so.'

Jeremiah 33:10 THE MESSAGE

'No weapon formed against you shall prosper, and every tongue which rises against you in judgment, you shall condemn. This is the heritage of the servant's of the LORD, and their righteousness is from Me,' says the LORD.

Isaiah 54:17 NKJV

For the Son of Man came to find and restore the lost.

Luke 19:9 THE MESSAGE

At that very time, Jesus cured many people of their diseases, illnesses, and evil spirits, and He restored sight to many who were blind.

Luke 7:21 NLT

But in our time something new has been added. What Moses and the prophets witnessed to all those years has happened. The God-setting-things-right that we read about has become Jesus- setting-things-right for us. And not only for us, but for everyone who believes in Him. For there is no difference between us and them in this. Since we've compiled this long and sorry record as sinners (both us and them) and proved that we are utterly incapable of living the glorious lives God wills for us, God did it for us. Out of sheer generosity He put us in right standing with Himself. A pure gift. He got us out of the mess we're in and restored us to where He always wanted us to be. And He did it by means of Jesus Christ.

Romans 3:21 THE MESSAGE

You shall write on them all the words of this law, when you have crossed over, that you may enter the land which the LORD your God is giving you, a land flowing with milk and honey, just as the LORD God of your fathers promised you.

Deuteronomy 27:3 NKJV

God, pick up the pieces. Put me back together again. You are my praise! Listen to how they talk about me...I never wanted trouble. You know what I've said. It's all out in the open before You. Don't add to my troubles. Give me some relief! Let those who harass me be harassed, not me. Let them be disgraced, not me.

Jeremiah 17:14-18 THE MESSAGE

As far as the east is from the west, so far has He removed our transgressions from us.

Psalm 103:12 NKJV

Therefore if the Son makes you free, you shall be free indeed.

John 8:36 NKJV

It wasn't so long ago that we ourselves were stupid and stubborn, dupes of sin, ordered every which way by our glands, going around with a chip on our shoulder, hated and hating back. But when God, our kind and loving Savior God, stepped in, He saved us from all that. It was all His doing; we had nothing to do with it. He gave us a good bath, and we came out of it new people, washed inside and out by the Holy Spirit. Our Savior Jesus poured out new life so generously. God's gift has restored our relationship with Him and given us back our lives. And there's more life to come - an eternity of life! You can count on this.

Titus 3:3 THE MESSAGE

Therefore, if anyone is in Christ, he is a new creation; old things have passed away; behold, all things have become new. Now all things are of God, who has reconciled us to Himself through Jesus Christ, and has given us the ministry of reconciliation, that is, that God was in Christ reconciling the world to Himself, not imputing their trespasses to them, and has committed to us the word of reconciliation.

2 Corinthians 5:17-19 NKJV

But from there you will seek the LORD your God, and you will find Him if you seek Him with all your heart and with all your soul. When you are in distress, and all these things come upon you in the latter days, when you turn to the LORD your God and obey His voice, for the LORD your

God is a merciful God. He will not forsake you nor destroy you, nor forget the covenant of your fathers which He swore to them.

Deuteronomy 4:29-31 NKJV

Then Jesus placed His hands on the man's eyes again, and his eyes were opened. His sight was completely restored, and he could see everything clearly.

Mark 8:25 NLT

The LORD also will be a refuge for the oppressed. A refuge in times of trouble, and those who know Your Name will put their trust in You. For You, LORD, have not forsaken those who seek You.

Psalm 9:9-10 NKJV

I will not leave you orphans; I will come to you.

fJohn 14:18 NKJV

The angel shows kindness, commanding death to release us, because the price was paid. Our health is restored, we feel young again, and we ask God to accept us. Then we joyfully worship God, and we are rewarded because we are innocent.

Job 33:24-26 CEV

'Believe Me, I've chosen and sanctified this Temple that you have built: My Name is stamped on it forever; My eyes are on it and My heart in it always. As for you, if you live in My presence as your father David lived, pure in heart and action, living the life I've set out for you, attentively obedient to My guidance and judgments, then I'll back your kingly rule over Israel - make it a sure thing on a sure foundation.'

2 Chronicles 7:12 THE MESSAGE

Restore to me the joy of Your salvation, and uphold me by Your generous Spirit.

Psalm 51:12 NKJV

Judah and Israel are like trees with branches broken by their enemies. But the LORD is going to restore their power and glory.

Nahum 2:2 CEV

This is the kind of fast day I'm after: to break the chains of injustice, get rid of exploitation in the workplace, free the oppressed, cancel debts. What I'm interested in seeing you do is: sharing your food with the hungry, inviting the homeless poor into your homes, putting clothes on the shivering ill-clad, being available to your own families. Do this and the lights will turn on, and your lives will turn around at once. Your righteousness will pave your way. The God of glory will secure your passage. Then when you pray, God will answer. You'll call out for help and I'll say, 'Here I am.' 'A Full Life in the Emptiest of Places' if you get rid of unfair practices, quit blaming victims, quit gossiping about other people's sins. If you are generous with the hungry and start giving yourselves to the down-and-out, your lives will begin to glow in the darkness, your shadowed lives will be bathed in sunlight. I will always show you where to go. I'll give you a full life in the emptiest of places - firm muscles, strong bones. You'll be like a well-watered garden, a gurgling spring that never runs dry. You'll use the old rubble of past lives to build anew, rebuild the foundations from out of your past. You'll be known as those who can fix anything, restore old ruins, rebuild and renovate, make the community livable again.

Isaiah 58:8-10 THE MESSAGE

The LORD is my rock, my fortress and my deliverer; my God is my rock, in Whom I take refuge, my shield and the horn of my salvation. He is my stronghold, my refuge and my Savior.

2 Samuel 22:2-3 NIV

But now, thus says the LORD, Who created you...and He Who formed you, 'Fear not, for I have redeemed you. I have called you by your name. You are Mine.'

Isaiah 43:1 NKJV

After Job had interceded for his friends, GOD restored his fortune – and then doubled it! All his brothers and sisters and friends came to his house and celebrated. They told him how sorry they were, and consoled him...each of them brought generous housewarming gifts.

Job 42:10-11 THE MESSAGE

Then He said to the man, 'Hold out your hand.' So the man held out his hand, and it was restored, just like the other one!

Matthew 12:13 NLT

Blessed be the God and Father of our Lord Jesus Christ, who has blessed us with every spiritual blessing in the heavenly places in Christ, just as He chose us in Him before the foundation of the world, that we would be holy and blameless before Him. In love He predestined us to adoption as sons through Jesus Christ to Himself, according to the kind intention of His will, to the praise of the glory of His grace, which He freely bestowed on us in the Beloved. In Him, we have redemption through His blood, the forgiveness of our trespasses, according to the riches of His grace which He lavished on us.

Ephesians 1:3-8 NASB

God appeared to Solomon that very night and said, 'I accept your prayer...[If] my...people respond by humbling themselves, praying, seeking My presence, and turning their backs on their wicked lives, I'll be there ready for you: I'll listen from heaven, forgive their sins, and restore their land to health. From now on I'm alert day and night to the prayers offered at this place. 'I AM the First, and I AM the Last. Besides Me, there is no God.'

2 Chronicles 7:12-18 THE MESSAGE

Do not be conformed to this world, this age, fashioned after and adapted to its external, superficial customs, but be transformed, changed, by the entire renewal of your mind by its new ideals and its new attitude, so that you may prove for yourselves, what is the good and acceptable and perfect will of God, even the thing which is good and acceptable and perfect in His sight for you.

Romans 12:2 AMP

I'll refresh tired bodies; I'll restore tired souls.

Jeremiah 31:25 THE MESSAGE

'I will restore everything that was lost.' God's Decree.

Jeremiah 32:42 THE MESSAGE

The LORD is close to all who call on Him, yes, to all who call on Him in truth.

Psalm 145:18 NLT

But now take another look. I'm going to give this city a thorough renovation, working a true healing inside and out. I'm going to show them life whole, life brimming with blessings. I'll restore everything that was lost to Judah and Jerusalem. I'll build everything back as good as new. I'll scrub them clean from the dirt they've done against Me. I'll forgive everything they've done wrong, forgive all their rebellions. And Jerusalem will be a center of joy and praise and glory for all the countries on earth. They'll get reports on all the good I'M doing for

*her. They'll be in awe of the blessings I AM pouring on
her.*

Jeremiah 33:6-9 THE MESSAGE

*Are you hurting? Pray. Do you feel great? Sing. Are you
sick? Call the church leaders together to pray and anoint
you with oil in the name of the Master. Believing-prayer
will heal you, and Jesus will put you on your feet. And if
you've sinned, you'll be forgiven - healed inside and out.
Make this your common practice: Confess your sins to
each other and pray for each other so that you can live
together whole and healed. The prayer of a person living
right with God is something powerful to be reckoned
with. Elijah, for instance, human just like us, prayed hard
that it wouldn't rain, and it didn't - not a drop for three
and a half years. Then he prayed that it would rain, and
it did. The showers came and everything started growing
again. My dear friends, if you know people who have
wandered off from God's truth, don't write them off. Go
after them. Get them back and you will have rescued
precious lives from destruction and prevented an
epidemic of wandering away from God.*

James 5:13-20 THE MESSAGE

*Here's what will happen...[if] you and your children take
[God's Word] seriously and come back to God, your God,
and obey Him with your whole heart and soul...God, your
God, will restore everything you lost; He'll have
compassion on you; He'll come back and pick up the
pieces from all the places where you were scattered. No
matter how far away you end up, God, your God, will get
you out of there and bring you back to the land your
ancestors once possessed. It will be yours again. He will
give you a good life and make you more numerous than
your ancestors.*

Deuteronomy 30:1 THE MESSAGE

Salvation

To rejoice knowing that I am saved and will live with God forever

Whoever calls upon the name of the LORD shall be saved.

Romans 10:13 NKJV

For God so greatly loved and dearly prized the world that He even gave up His only begotten Son, so that whoever believes in, trusts in, clings to, relies on Him shall not perish, come to destruction, be lost, but have eternal everlasting life. For God did not sent His Son into the world in order to judge, to reject, to condemn, to pass sentence on the world, but that the world might find salvation and be made safe and sound through Him.

John 3:16-17 AMP

Thanks be to God for His indescribable Gift, Jesus Christ.

2 Corinthians 9:15 NKJV

Also at that time, people will say, 'Look at what's happened! This is our God! We waited for Him and He showed up and saved us! This God, the One we waited for!

Let's celebrate, sing the joys of His salvation. God's hand rests on this mountain!'

Isaiah 25:9 THE MESSAGE

'I, yes I, AM God. I'M the only Savior there is. I spoke, I saved, I told you what existed long before these upstart gods appeared on the scene. And you know it, you're my witnesses, you're the evidence.' God's Decree. 'Yes, I AM God. I've always been God and I always will be God. No one can take anything from Me. I make; who can unmake it?'

Isaiah 46:8 THE MESSAGE

This is the testimony in essence: God gave us eternal life; the life is in His Son. So, whoever has the Son, has life; whoever rejects the Son, rejects life. My purpose in writing is simply this: that you who believe in God's Son will know beyond the shadow of a doubt that you have eternal life, the reality and not the illusion. And how bold and free we then become in His presence, freely asking according to His will, sure that He's listening. And if we're confident that He's listening, we know that what we've asked for is as good as ours.

1 John 5:11-13 THE MESSAGE

Souls are saved by truthful witness and betrayed by the spread of lies.

Proverbs 14:25 THE MESSAGE

Jesus said, 'Go ahead - see again! Your faith has saved and healed you!' The healing was instant: He looked up, seeing - and then followed Jesus, glorifying God. Everyone in the street joined in, shouting praise to God.

Luke 18:42 THE MESSAGE

I sing to God, the Praise-Lofty, and find myself safe and saved... But me He caught - reached all the way from sky to sea; He pulled me out of that ocean of hate, that enemy chaos, the void in which I was drowning. They hit me when I was down, but God stuck by me. He stood me up on a wide-open field; I stood there saved - surprised to be loved!

Psalm 18:3, 16 THE MESSAGE

Come, let's shout praises to God, raise the roof for the Rock who saved us! Let's march into His presence singing praises, lifting the rafters with our hymns!

Psalm 95:1 THE MESSAGE

'On your way,' said Jesus. 'Your faith has saved and healed you.' In that very instant he recovered his sight and followed Jesus down the road.

Mark 10:52 THE MESSAGE

Clearly, you are a God who works behind the scenes, God of Israel, Savior God. Humiliated, all those others will be ashamed to show their faces in public. Out of work and at loose ends, the makers of no-god idols won't know what to do with themselves. The people of Israel, though, are saved by You, God - saved with an eternal salvation. They won't be ashamed, they won't be at loose ends, ever.

Isaiah 45:15 THE MESSAGE

I'M still your God, the God who saved you out of Egypt. I'M the only real God you've ever known. I'M the One and only God Who delivers. I took care of you during the wilderness hard times, those years when you had nothing. I took care of you, took care of all your needs, gave you everything you needed. You were spoiled. You thought you didn't need Me. You forgot Me.

Hosea 13:4-6 THE MESSAGE

*He saved you from that hard life surrounded by enemies,
and you lived in peace.*

1 Samuel 12:11 THE MESSAGE

*But God stepped in and saved me from certain death. I'm
alive again! Once more I see the light!*

Job 33:26 THE MESSAGE

*And she will bring forth a Son, and you shall call His
name Jesus, for He will save His people from their sins.*

Matthew 1:21 NKJV

*What you say goes, God, and stays, as permanent as the
heavens. Your truth never goes out of fashion; it's as up-
to-date as the earth when the sun comes up. Your Word
and truth are dependable as ever; that's what You
ordered - You set the earth going. If Your revelation
hadn't delighted me so, I would have given up when the
hard times came. But I'll never forget the advice You gave
me; You saved my life with those wise words. Save me!
I'm all Yours. I look high and low for Your words of
wisdom. The wicked lie in ambush to destroy me, but I'm
only concerned with Your plans for me. I see the limits to
everything human, but the horizons can't contain Your
commands!*

Psalm 119:89 THE MESSAGE

*I love God because He listened to me, listened as I begged
for mercy. He listened so intently as I laid out my case
before Him. Death stared me in the face, hell was hard on
my heels. Up against it, I didn't know which way to turn;
then I called out to God for help: 'Please, God!' I cried out.
'Save my life!' God is gracious—it is He who makes things
right, our most compassionate God. God takes the side of
the helpless; when I was at the end of my rope, He saved
me.*

Psalm 116:1 THE MESSAGE

[Jesus] ignored them and said to the woman, 'Your faith has saved you. Go in peace.'

Luke 7:50 THE MESSAGE

Then He said, 'Go into the world. Go everywhere and announce the Message of God's good news to one and all. Whoever believes and is baptized is saved; whoever refuses to believe is damned.'

Mark 16:14 THE MESSAGE

The God of my father is my help and saved me from death by Pharaoh.

Exodus 18:1 THE MESSAGE

He wants not only us but everyone saved, you know, everyone to get to know the truth we've learned: that there's one God and only One, and one Priest- Mediator between God and us - Jesus, Who offered Himself in exchange for everyone held captive by sin, to set them all free. Eventually the news is going to get out. This and this only has been my appointed work: getting this news to those who have never heard of God, and explaining how it works by simple faith and plain truth.

1 Timothy 2:4 THE MESSAGE

There is one body, one Spirit, one hope, one Lord, one faith, one baptism, one God, and one Father of all Who is above all.

Ephesians 4:4-5 NKJV

I sing to God the Praise-Lofty, and find myself safe and saved.

2 Samuel 22:4 THE MESSAGE

Can plunder be retrieved from a giant, prisoners of war gotten back from a tyrant? But God says, 'Even if a giant grips the plunder and a tyrant holds my people prisoner,

I'M the one Who's on your side, defending your cause, rescuing your children. And your enemies, crazed and desperate, will turn on themselves, killing each other in a frenzy of self-destruction. Then everyone will know that I, God, have saved you - I, the Mighty One of Jacob.'

Isaiah 49:24 THE MESSAGE

He has delivered us from the power of darkness and conveyed us into the kingdom of the Son of His love, in Whom we have redemption through His blood, the forgiveness of sins.

Colossians 1:13-14 NKJV

So don't be embarrassed to speak up for our Master or for me, His prisoner. Take your share of suffering for the Message along with the rest of us. We can only keep on going, after all, by the power of God, Who first saved us and then called us to this holy work. We had nothing to do with it. It was all His idea, a gift prepared for us in Jesus long before we knew anything about it. But we know it now. Since the appearance of our Savior, nothing could be plainer: death defeated, life vindicated in a steady blaze of light, all through the work of Jesus.

2 Timothy 1:8 THE MESSAGE

No one who does evil can be saved by evil.

Ecclesiastes 8:8 THE MESSAGE

Now God has us where He wants us, with all the time in this world and the next to shower grace and kindness upon us in Christ Jesus. Saving is all His idea, and all His work. All we do is trust Him enough to let Him do it. It's God's gift from start to finish! We don't play the major role. If we did, we'd probably go around bragging that we'd done the whole thing! No, we neither make nor save ourselves. God does both the making and saving. He creates each of us by Christ Jesus to join Him in the work

He does, the good work He has gotten ready for us to do, work we had better be doing.

Ephesians 2:7-10 THE MESSAGE

...That having been justified by His grace we should become heirs according to the hope of eternal life.

Titus 3:7 NKJV

Walk straight - live well and be saved; a devious life is a doomed life.

Proverbs 28:18 THE MESSAGE

The LORD is my light and my salvation; whom shall I fear? The LORD is the strength of my life; of whom shall I be afraid?

Psalm 27:1 NKJV

They replied, 'Believe in the Lord Jesus, and you will be saved – you and your household.'

Acts 16:31 NKJV

STRENGTH

When I am weak and need God's power over my situation

Let us then approach the throne of grace with confidence, so that we may receive mercy and find grace to help us in our time of need.

Hebrews 4:16 NIV

The everlasting God, the LORD, the Creator of the ends of the earth, neither faints nor is weary. His understanding is unsearchable. He gives power to the weak, and to those who have no might He increases strength.

Isaiah 40:28-29 NKJV

Guard My common good: do what's right and do it in the right way, for salvation is just around the corner, My setting-things-right is about to go into action. How blessed are you who enter into these things, you men and women who embrace them.

Isaiah 56:1-2 THE MESSAGE

Wait on the LORD; Be of good courage, and He shall strengthen your heart; Wait, I say, on the LORD!

Psalm 27:14 NKJV

193

These things I have spoken to you while being present with you. But the Helper, the Holy Spirit Whom the Father will send in My Name, He will teach you all things and bring to your remembrance all things that I said to you.

John 14:25-26 NKJV

Finally, brethren, we urge and exhort in the Lord Jesus that you should abound more and more, just as you received from us how you ought to walk and to please God.

1 Thessalonians 4:1 NKJV

Finally, brethren, farewell and rejoice! Be strengthened, perfected, completed, made what you ought to be, be encouraged, and consoled and comforted; be of the same mind, one with another; live in peace, and then the God of love, Who is the Source of affection, goodwill, love and benevolence toward men and the Author and Promoter of peace will be with you.

2 Corinthians 13:11 AMP

So shall My Word be that goes forth from My mouth; it shall not return to Me void, but it shall accomplish what I please, and it shall prosper in the thing for which I sent it.

Isaiah 53:5 NKJV

Everyone helped his neighbor, and said to his brother, 'be of good courage!'

Isaiah 41:6 NKJV

Draw near to God and He will draw near to you.

James 4:8 NKJV

Then your light shall dawn in the darkness, and your darkness shall be as the noonday. The LORD will guide you continually, and satisfy your soul in drought, and strengthen your bones; you shall be like a watered garden and like a spring of water, whose waters do not fail.

Isaiah 58:10-11 NKJV

Blessed is the man who trusts in the LORD, and whose hope is the LORD. For he shall be like a tree planted by the waters, which spreads out its roots by the river, and will not fear when heat comes; but its leaf will be green, and will not be anxious in the year of drought, nor will cease from yielding fruit.

Jeremiah 17:7-8 NKJV

I AM with you always.

Matthew 28:20 NKJV

My sheep hear My voice, and I know them, and they follow Me. And I give them eternal life, and they shall never perish; neither shall anyone snatch them out of My Hand. My Father, who has given them to Me, is greater than all; and no one is able to snatch them out of My Father's Hand.

John 10:27-29 NKJV

When you pass through the waters, I will be with you. And through the rivers, they shall not overflow you. When you walk through the fire, you shall not be burned. Nor shall the flame scorch you. For I AM the LORD your God, the Holy One of Israel, your Savior...you have been honored, and I have loved you....fear not, for I AM with you.

Isaiah 43:2-4 NKJV

But I have trusted in Your mercy. My heart shall rejoice in Your salvation. I will sing to the LORD because He has dealt bountifully with me.

Psalm 13:5-6 NKJV

You are of God, little children, and have overcome them, because He who is in you is greater than he who is in the world.

1 John 4:4 NKJV

No temptation has overtaken you except such as is common to man; but God is faithful, Who will not allow you to be tempted beyond what you are able, but with the temptation will also make the way of escape, that you may be able to bear it.

1 Corinthians 10:13 NKJV

The LORD your God is with you wherever you go.

Joshua 1:9 NKJV

Mercy, peace, and love be multiplied to you.

Jude 1:2 NKJV

You then, my son, be strong in the grace that is in Christ Jesus.

2 Timothy 2:1 NIV

Now thanks be to God who always leads us in triumph in Christ, and through us, diffuses the fragrance of His knowledge in every place.

2 Corinthians 2:14 NKJV

And in their prayers for you their hearts will go out to you because of the surpassing grace God has given you.

2 Corinthians 9:14 NIV

For this is the love of God, that we keep His commandments. And His commandments are not burdensome. For whatever is born of God overcomes the world. And this is the victory that has overcome the world – our faith.

1 John 5:3-4 NKJV

But He said to me, 'My grace is sufficient for you, for My power is made perfect in weakness.' Therefore I will boast all the more gladly about my weaknesses, so that Christ's power may rest on me.

2 Corinthians 12:9 NIV

I thank Christ Jesus our Lord, Who has given me strength, that He considered me faithful, appointing me to His service.

1 Timothy 1:12 NIV

Be of good courage, and He shall strengthen your heart, all you who hope in the LORD.

Psalm 31:24 NKJV

The LORD is my light and my salvation; whom shall I fear? The LORD is the strength of my life; of whom shall I be afraid?

Psalm 27:1 NKJV

God is our refuge and strength, a very present help in trouble. Therefore, we will not fear, even though the earth be removed, and though the mountains be carried into the midst of the sea; though its waters roar and be troubled, though the mountains shake with its swelling.

Psalm 46:1-3 NKJV

Success

To know what my true wealth and accomplishments are

For God is not unjust to forget your work and labor of love which you have shown toward His Name...

Hebrews 6:10 NKJV

There are precious treasures and oil in the dwelling of the wise, but a foolish man swallows it up. He who pursues righteousness and loyalty finds life, righteousness and honor....he who guards his mouth and his tongue guards his soul from troubles.

Proverbs 21:20-21, 23 NASB

Whoever trusts in his riches will fall, but the righteous will thrive like a green leaf.

Proverbs 11:28 NIV

And let us consider one another in order to stir up love and good works.

Hebrews 10:24 NKJV

And you shall remember the LORD your God, for it is He Who gives you power to get wealth, that He may establish His covenant which He swore to your fathers, as it is this day.

Deuteronomy 8:18 NKJV

Ho! Everyone who thirsts, come to the waters; and you who have no money, come, buy and eat. Yes, come, buy wine and milk without money and without price. Why do you spend money for what is not bread? And your wages for what does not satisfy? Listen carefully to Me, and eat what is good, and let your soul delight itself in abundance. Incline your ear and come to Me. Hear and your soul shall live, and I will make an everlasting covenant with you.

Isaiah 55:1-3 NKJV

For God has not given us a spirit of fear, but of power and of love and of a sound mind.

2 Timothy 1:7 NKJV

Every good and perfect gift is from above, coming down from the Father of the lights, with Whom there is no variation or shadow of turning.

James 1:17 NKJV

And He will love you and bless you and multiply you; He will also bless the fruit of your womb and the fruit of your land, your grain, and your new wine and your oil, the increase of your cattle, and the offspring of your flock, in the land of which He swore to your fathers to give you.

Deuteronomy 7:13 NKJV

John answered, 'It's not possible for a person to succeed - I'm talking about eternal success - without heaven's help.'

John 3:27 THE MESSAGE

The blessing of the LORD makes one rich, and He adds no sorrow to it.

Proverbs 10:22 NKJV

By this My Father is glorified, that you bear much fruit; so you will be My disciples.

John 15:8 NKJV

I can't tell you how much I long for you to enter this wide-open, spacious life. We didn't fence you in. The smallness you feel comes from within you. Your lives aren't small, but you're living them in a small way. I'm speaking as plainly as I can and with great affection. Open up your lives. Live openly and expansively!

2 Corinthians 6:11-13 THE MESSAGE

My purpose is that they may be encouraged in heart and united in love, so that they may have the full riches of complete understanding in order that they may know the mystery of God, namely, Christ Jesus, in Whom are hidden all the treasures of wisdom and knowledge.

Colossians 2:2-3 NIV

Whoever can be trusted with very little can also be trusted with much, and whoever is dishonest with very little will also be dishonest with much. So if you have not been trustworthy in handling worldly wealth, who will trust you with true riches? And if you have not been trustworthy with someone else's property, who will give you property of your own?

Luke 16:10-12 NIV

A good name is rather to be chosen than great riches, and loving favor rather than silver and gold. The rich and poor meet together; the Lord is the Maker of them all. A prudent man sees the evil and hides himself, but the simple, pass on and are punished. The reward of humility and the reverent and worshipful awe of the Lord is riches and honor and life.

Proverbs 22:1-4 AMP

Honor the LORD with your possessions, and with the first fruits of all your increase; so your barns will be filled with plenty and your vats will overflow with new wine.

Proverbs 3:9-10 NKJV

Give, and it will be given to you; good measure, pressed down, shaken together and running over will be put into your bosom. For with the same measure that you use, it will be measured back to you.

Luke 6:38 NKJV

Hezekiah carried out this work and kept it up everywhere in Judah. He was the very best - good, right, and true before his God. Everything he took up, whether it had to do with worship in God's Temple or the carrying out of God's Law and Commandments, he did well in a spirit of prayerful worship. He was a great success.

2 Chronicles 31:20 THE MESSAGE

Now thanks be to God Who always leads us in triumph in Christ, and through us, diffuses the fragrance of His knowledge in every place.

2 Corinthians 2:14 NKJV

Here is a simple, rule-of-thumb guide for behavior: Ask yourself what you want people to do for you, then grab the initiative and do it for them. Add up God's Law and Prophets and this is what you get. Don't look for shortcuts to God. The market is flooded with surefire, easygoing formulas for a successful life that can be practiced in your spare time. Don't fall for that stuff, even though crowds of people do. The way to life - to God! - is vigorous and requires total attention.

Matthew 7: 12-14 THE MESSAGE

I will give you hidden treasures, riches stored in secret places, so that you may know that I AM the LORD, the God of Israel, Who summons you by name.

Isaiah 45:3 NKJV

You don't get wormy apples off a healthy tree, nor good apples off a diseased tree. The health of the apple tells the health of the tree. You must begin with your own life-giving lives. It's who you are, not what you say and do, that counts. Your true being brims over into true words and deeds.

Luke 6:43 THE MESSAGE

Appoint leaders in every town according to my instructions. As you select them, ask, Is this man well-thought-of? Is he committed to his wife? Are his children believers? Do they respect him and stay out of trouble? It's important that a church leader, responsible for the affairs in God's house, be looked up to - not pushy, not short-tempered, not a drunk, not a bully, not money-hungry. He must welcome people, be helpful, wise, fair, reverent, have a good grip on himself, and have a good grip on the Message, knowing how to use the truth to either spur people on in knowledge or stop them in their tracks if they oppose it. For there are a lot of rebels out there, full of loose, confusing, and deceiving talk. Those who were brought up religious and ought to know better are the worst. They've got to be shut up. They're disrupting entire families with their teaching, and all for the sake of a fast buck.

Titus 1:5-16 THE MESSAGE

So now, son, God be with you. God-speed as you build the sanctuary for your God, the job God has given you. And may God also give you discernment and understanding when he puts you in charge of Israel so that you will rule in reverent obedience under God's Revelation. That's what will make you successful, following the directions and doing the things that God commanded Moses for Israel. Courage! Take charge! Don't be timid; don't hold back. Look at this - I've gone to a lot of trouble to stockpile materials for the sanctuary of God: a hundred thousand talents (3,775 tons) of gold, a million talents (37,750 tons) of silver, tons of bronze and iron - too much to weigh - and all this timber and stone. And you're free to add more. And workers both plentiful and prepared: stonecutters, masons, carpenters, artisans in gold and silver, bronze and iron. You're all set - get to work! And God-speed!

1 Chronicles 22:11 THE MESSAGE

May the LORD God of your fathers make you a thousand times more numerous than you are, and bless you as He has promised you!

Deuteronomy 1:11 NKJV

Beloved, I pray that you may prosper in all things and be in health, just as your soul prospers.

3 John 2 NKJV

Do you want to be counted wise, to build a reputation for wisdom? Here's what you do: Live well, live wisely, live humbly. It's the way you live, not the way you talk, that counts. Mean- spirited ambition isn't wisdom. Boasting that you are wise isn't wisdom. Twisting the truth to make yourselves sound wise isn't wisdom. It's the furthest thing from wisdom—it's animal cunning, devilish conniving. Whenever you're trying to look better than others or get the better of others, things fall apart and everyone ends up at the others' throats. Real wisdom, God's wisdom, begins with a holy life and is characterized by getting along with others. It is gentle and reasonable, overflowing with mercy and blessings, not hot one day and cold the next, not two-faced. *You can develop a healthy, robust community that lives right with God and enjoy its results only if you do the hard work of getting along with each other, treating each other with dignity and honor.*

James 3:13-18 THE MESSAGE

TRUTH

To know the truth in each of life's situations through the unfailing timelessness of God's Word

We refuse to wear masks and play games. We don't maneuver and manipulate behind the scenes. And we don't twist God's Word to suit ourselves. Rather, we keep everything we do and say out in the open, the whole truth on display, so that those who want to can see and judge for themselves in the presence of God... If our Message is obscure to anyone, it's not because we're holding back in any way. No, it's because these other people are looking or going the wrong way and refuse to give it serious attention. All they have eyes for is the fashionable god of darkness. They think he can give them what they want, and that they won't have to bother believing a Truth they can't see. They're stone- blind to the dayspring brightness of the Message that shines with Christ, who gives us the best picture of God we'll ever get.

2 Corinthians 4:1, 3 THE MESSAGE

Every word of God is pure; He is a shield to those who put their trust in Him.

Proverbs 30:5 NKJV

All Scripture is given by inspiration of God, and is profitable and useful to teach us what is true and to make us realize what is wrong in our lives. It straightens us out and teaches us to do what is right.

2 Timothy 3:16 NLT

Then, when he prayed again, the sky sent down rain and the earth began to yield its crops. My dear brothers and sisters, if someone among you wanders away from the truth and is brought back, you can be sure that whoever brings the sinner back will save that person from death and bring about the forgiveness of many sins.

James 5:18-20 NLT

The answer's simple: Live right, speak the truth, despise exploitation, refuse bribes, reject violence, avoid evil amusements. This is how you raise your standard of living! A safe and stable way to live, a nourishing, satisfying way to live.

Isaiah 33:15 THE MESSAGE

A lying witness is unconvincing; a person who speaks truth is respected.

Proverbs 21:28 THE MESSAGE

Can a fig tree produce olives or a grapevine produce figs? Does fresh water come from a well full of salt water? Are any of you wise or sensible? Then show it by living right and by being humble and wise in everything you do. But if your heart is full of bitter jealousy and selfishness, don't brag or lie to cover up the truth.

James 3:12-14 THE MESSAGE

'Because you're not yet taking God seriously,' said Jesus. 'The simple truth is that if you had a mere kernel of faith, a poppy seed, say, you would tell this mountain, 'Move!'

*and it would move. There is nothing you wouldn't be able
to tackle.'*

Matthew 17:20 THE MESSAGE

*The whole point of what we're urging is simply love - love
uncontaminated by self-interest and counterfeit faith, a
life open to God. Those who fail to keep to this point soon
wander off into cul-de-sacs of gossip. They set themselves
up as experts on religious issues, but haven't the remotest
idea of what they're holding forth with such imposing
eloquence. It's true that moral guidance and counsel
need to be given, but the way you say it and to whom you
say it are as important as what you say. It's obvious, isn't
it, that the law code isn't primarily for people who live
responsibly, but for the irresponsible, who defy all
authority, riding roughshod over God, life, sex, truth,
whatever! They are contemptuous of this great Message
I've been put in charge of by this great God.*

1 Timothy 1:5-11 THE MESSAGE

*Thomas said, 'Master, we have no idea where you're
going. How do you expect us to know the road?' Jesus
said, 'I AM the Road, also the Truth, also the Life. No one
gets to the Father apart from Me. If you really knew Me,
you would know My Father as well. From now on, you do
know Him. You've even seen Him!'*

John 14:5-7 THE MESSAGE

*Put on your new nature, created to be like God - truly
righteous and holy. So stop telling lies. Let us tell our
neighbors the truth, for we are all parts of the same body.
And 'don't sin by letting anger control you.' Don't let the
sun go down while you are still angry, for anger gives a
foothold to the devil. If you are a thief, quit stealing.
Instead, use your hands for good hard work, and then
give generously to others in need.*

Ephesians 4:24-28 NLT

Now that you've cleaned up your lives by following the truth, love one another as if your lives depended on it. Your new life is not like your old life.

1 Peter 1:22 THE MESSAGE

He will answer them, 'I'M telling the solemn truth: Whenever you failed to [care for] someone who was being overlooked or ignored, that was Me - you failed to do it to Me.'

Matthew 25:45 THE MESSAGE

I've written to warn you about those who are trying to deceive you. But they're no match for what is embedded deeply within you - Christ's anointing, no less! You don't need any of their so-called teaching. Christ's anointing teaches you the truth on everything you need to know about yourself and Him, uncontaminated by a single lie. Live deeply in what you were taught.

1 John 2:26 THE MESSAGE

The Spirit makes it clear that as time goes on, some are going to give up on the faith and chase after demonic illusions put forth by professional liars. These liars have lied so well and for so long that they've lost their capacity for truth. They will tell you not to get married. They'll tell you not to eat this or that food - perfectly good food God created to be eaten heartily and with thanksgiving by believers who know better! Everything God created is good, and to be received with thanks. Nothing is to be sneered at and thrown out. God's Word and our prayers make every item in creation holy.

1 Timothy 4:1-5 THE MESSAGE

Jesus told the people who had faith in Him, 'If you keep on obeying what I have said, you truly are My disciples. You will know the truth, and the truth will set you free.'

John 8:31 CEV

Good leaders cultivate honest speech; they love advisors who tell them the truth.

Proverbs 16:13 THE MESSAGE

The law of the LORD is perfect, converting the soul. The testimony of the LORD is sure, making wise the simple. The statutes of the LORD are right, rejoicing the heart. The commandment of the LORD is pure, enlightening the eyes. The fear of the LORD is clean, enduring forever. The judgments of the LORD are true and righteous altogether. More to be desired are they than gold. Yea, than much fine gold, sweeter also than honey and the honeycomb. Moreover by them, Your servant is taught, and in keeping them there is great reward.

Psalm 19:7-11 NKJV

All is nothing compared to You, O God. You are wondrously great, famously great...Look far and wide among the elite of the nations. The best they can come up with is nothing compared to You...but God is the real thing – the living God, the eternal King... it is God whose power made the earth, whose wisdom gave shape to the world, who crafted the cosmos. He thunders, and rain pours down. He sends the clouds soaring, He embellishes the storm with lightning, launches wind from His warehouse.

Jeremiah 10: 6-8, 10-13 THE MESSAGE

From there [Jesus] went all over Galilee. He used synagogues for meeting places and taught people the truth of God. God's kingdom was His theme - that beginning right now they were under God's government, a good government! He also healed people of their diseases and of the bad effects of their bad lives.

Matthew 4:23 THE MESSAGE

Woe to you who turn justice to vinegar and stomp righteousness into the mud. Do you realize where you are? You're in a cosmos star-flung with constellations by God, a world God wakes up each morning and puts to bed each night. God dips water from the ocean and gives the land a drink. God, God-revealed, does all this. And He can destroy it as easily as make it. He can turn this vast wonder into total waste. People hate this kind of talk. Raw truth is never popular, but here it is, bluntly spoken: Because you run roughshod over the poor and take the bread right out of their mouths, you're never going to move into the luxury homes you have built. You're never going to drink wine from the expensive vineyards you've planted. I know precisely the extent of your violations, the enormity of your sins. Appalling! You bully right-living people, taking bribes right and left and kicking the poor when they're down. Justice is a lost cause. Evil is epidemic. Decent people throw up their hands. Protest and rebuke are useless, a waste of breath. Seek good and not evil - and live! You talk about God, the God-of-the-Angel- Armies, being your best friend. Well, live like it, and maybe it will happen. Hate evil and love good, then work it out in the public square. Maybe God, the God-of-the-Angel-Armies, will notice your remnant and be gracious.

Amos 5:7-15 THE MESSAGE

Peter fairly exploded with his good news: 'It's God's own truth, nothing could be plainer: God plays no favorites! It makes no difference who you are or where you're from - if you want God and are ready to do as He says, the door is open.'

Acts 10:34 THE MESSAGE

These are the things I want you to teach and preach. If you have leaders there who teach otherwise, who refuse the solid words of our Master Jesus and this Godly instruction, tag them for what they are: ignorant windbags who infect the air with germs of envy, controversy, bad- mouthing, suspicious rumors. Eventually there's an epidemic of backstabbing, and truth is but a distant memory. They think religion is a way to make a fast buck.

1 Timothy 6:2-5 THE MESSAGE

There's nothing like the written Word of God for showing you the way to salvation through faith in Christ Jesus. Every part of Scripture is God- breathed and useful one way or another - showing us truth, exposing our rebellion, correcting our mistakes, training us to live God's way. Through the Word we are put together and shaped up for the tasks God has for us.

2 Timothy 3:14 THE MESSAGE

Sanctify them by Your truth. Your Word is truth.

John 17:17 NIV

The best that can be said for it is that the testing process will bring truth into the open and confirm it.

1 Corinthians 11:17 THE MESSAGE

...God Himself is the truth.

John 3:31 THE MESSAGE

They are going to do all these things to you because of the way they treated Me, because they don't know the One Who sent Me. If I hadn't come and told them all this in plain language, it wouldn't be so bad. As it is, they have no excuse. Hate Me, hate My Father - it's all the same. If I hadn't done what I have done among them, works no-one has ever done, they wouldn't be to blame. But they saw the God-signs and hated anyway, both Me and my Father. Interesting, they have verified the truth of their own Scriptures where it is written, 'They hated Me for no good reason'...when the Friend I plan to send you from the Father comes - the Spirit of Truth issuing from the Father - He will confirm everything about Me. You, too, from your side must give your confirming evidence, since you are in this with Me from the start.

John 15:21, 26 THE MESSAGE

'Don't be afraid. And now here's what I want you to do: Tell the truth, the whole truth, when you speak. Do the right thing by one another, both personally and in your courts. Don't cook up plans to take unfair advantage of others. Don't do or say what so isn't. I hate all that stuff. Keep your lives simple and honest.' Decree of God...Embrace truth! Love peace!

Zechariah 8:14, 18 THE MESSAGE

Jesus said to His disciples: 'If you love Me, you will do as I command. Then I will ask the Father to send you the Holy Spirit who will help you and always be with you.'

John 14:14-16 CEV

I still have many things to tell you, but you can't handle them now. But when the Friend comes, the Spirit of the Truth, He will take you by the hand and guide you into all the truth there is. He won't draw attention to Himself, but will make sense out of what is about to happen and, indeed, out of all that I have done and said.

John 16:12 THE MESSAGE

The world is unprincipled. It's dog-eat-dog out there! The world doesn't fight fair. But we don't live or fight our battles that way - never have and never will. The tools of our trade aren't for marketing or manipulation, but they are for demolishing that entire massively corrupt culture. We use our powerful God- tools for smashing warped philosophies, tearing down barriers erected against the truth of God, fitting every loose thought and emotion and impulse into the structure of life shaped by Christ. Our tools are ready at hand for clearing the ground of every obstruction and building lives of obedience into maturity.

2 Corinthians 10:3 THE MESSAGE

This is the crisis we're in: God-light streamed into the world, but men and women everywhere ran for the darkness. They went for the darkness because they were not really interested in pleasing God. Everyone who makes a practice of doing evil, addicted to denial and illusion, hates God-light and won't come near it, fearing a painful exposure. But anyone working and living in truth and reality welcomes God-light so the work can be seen for the God-work it is.

John 3:19 THE MESSAGE

And he answered and said, 'I believe that Jesus Christ is the Son of God.'

Acts 8:37 NKJV

Not only that - count yourselves blessed every time people put you down or throw you out or speak lies about you to discredit Me. What it means is that the truth is too close for comfort and they are uncomfortable. You can be glad when that happens - give a cheer, even! - for though they don't like it, I do! And all heaven applauds. And know that you are in good company. My prophets and witnesses have always gotten into this kind of trouble.

Matthew 5:11-12 THE MESSAGE

My covenant with Levi was to give life and peace. I kept my covenant with him, and he honored Me. He stood in reverent awe before Me. He taught the truth and did not lie. He walked with Me in peace and uprightness. He kept many out of the ditch, kept them on the road.

Malachi 2:4 THE MESSAGE

Then Pilate said, 'So, are you a king or not?' Jesus answered, 'You tell me. Because I am King, I was born and entered the world so that I could witness to the truth. Everyone who cares for truth, who has any feeling for the truth, recognizes My voice.'

John 18:37 THE MESSAGE

Most of all, try to proclaim His truth. If you praise Him in the private language of tongues, God understands you but no one else does, for you are sharing intimacies just between you and Him. But when you proclaim His truth in everyday speech, you're letting others in on the truth so that they can grow and be strong and experience His presence with you.

1 Corinthians 14:1 THE MESSAGE

Sitting across from the offering box, he was observing how the crowd tossed money in for the collection. Many of the rich were making large contributions. One poor widow came up and put in two small coins - a measly two cents. Jesus called His disciples over and said, 'The truth is that this poor widow gave more to the collection than all the others put together. All the others gave what they'll never miss; she gave extravagantly what she couldn't afford - she gave her all.'

Mark 12:41 THE MESSAGE

In the beginning was the Word, and the Word was with God, and the Word was God. He was in the beginning with God. All things were made through Him, and without Him, nothing was made that was made. In Him was life, and the life was the light of men. And the light shines in the darkness, and the darkness did not comprehend it.

John 1:1-5 NKJV

Love and truth form a good leader; sound leadership is founded on loving integrity.

Proverbs 20:28 THE MESSAGE

Count yourself blessed every time someone cuts you down or throws you out, every time someone smears or blackens your name to discredit Me. What it means is that the truth is too close for comfort and that that person is uncomfortable. You can be glad when that happens - skip like a lamb, if you like! - for even though they don't like it, I do . . . and all heaven applauds. And know that you are in good company; My preachers and witnesses have always been treated like this. There's trouble ahead when you live only for the approval of others, saying what flatters them, doing what indulges them. Popularity contests are not truth contests - look how many scoundrel preachers were approved by your ancestors! Your task is to be true, not popular. To you who are ready for the truth, I say this: Love your enemies. Let them bring out the best in you, not the worst. When someone gives you a hard time, respond with the energies of prayer for that person. If someone slaps you in the face, stand there and take it. If someone grabs your shirt, gift wrap your best coat and make a present of it. If someone takes unfair advantage of you, usethe occasion to practice the servant life. No more tit- for-tat stuff. Live generously.

Luke 6: 22, 26-27 THE MESSAGE

Truth lasts; lies are here today, gone tomorrow.

Proverbs 12:19 THE MESSAGE

The more talk, the less truth; the wise measure their words.

Proverbs 10:19 THE MESSAGE

Listen carefully to My wisdom; take to heart what I can teach you. You'll treasure its sweetness deep within; you'll give it bold expression in your speech. To make sure your foundation is solid, trust in God, I'm laying it all out right now just for you. I'm giving you thirty sterling principles - tested guidelines to live by. Believe me - these are truths that work, and will keep you accountable to those who sent you.

Proverbs 22:17 THE MESSAGE

Whatever I command you, be careful to observe it; you shall not add to it nor take away from it.

Deuteronomy 12:32 NKJV

If a prophet, or one who foretells by dreams, appears among you and announces to you a miraculous sign or wonder, and if the sign or wonder of which he has spoken takes place and he says, 'let us follow other gods (gods you have not known), and let us worship them,' you must not listen to the words of that prophet or dreamer. The LORD your God is testing you to find out whether you love Him with all your heart and with all your soul. It is the LORD your God, you must follow and Him you must revere. Keep His commands and obey Him; serve Him and hold fast to Him.

Deuteronomy 13:1-4 NIV

Do you hear Lady Wisdom calling? Can you hear Madame Insight raising her voice? She's taken her stand at First and Main, at the busiest intersection. Right in the city square where the traffic is thickest, she shouts, 'You - I'm talking to all of you, everyone out here on the streets! Listen...shape up! Don't miss a word of this - I'm telling you how to live well, I'm telling you how to live at your best. My mouth chews and savors and relishes truth - I can't stand the taste of evil! You'll only hear true and right words from my mouth; not one syllable will be twisted or skewed. You'll recognize this as true - you with open minds; truth-ready minds will see it at once. Prefer My life-disciplines over chasing after money, and God-knowledge over a lucrative career. For Wisdom is better than all the trappings of wealth; nothing you could wish for holds a candle to her.'

Proverbs 8:1 THE MESSAGE

Souls are saved by truthful witness and betrayed by the spread of lies.

Proverbs 14:25 THE MESSAGE

Jesus Christ, the Messiah, is always the same, yesterday, today, yes, and forever to the ages. Do not be carried about by different and varied and alien teachings; for it is good for the heart to be established and ennobled and strengthened by means of grace, God's favor and spiritual blessing, and not to be devoted to foods, rules of diet and ritualistic meals, which bring no spiritual benefit or profit to those who observe them.

Hebrews 13:8-9 AMP

Whoever slanders his neighbor in secret, him will I put to silence; whoever has haughty eyes and a proud heart, him will I not endure. My eyes will be on the faithful in the land, that they may dwell with Me; he whose walk is blameless will minister to Me. No one who practices deceit will dwell in My house; no one who speaks falsely will stand in my presence.

Psalm 101:5-7 NIV

Have I then become your enemy by telling the truth to you and dealing sincerely with you?

Galatians 4:16 AMP

And God's grace and truth go with you!

2 Samuel 15:19 THE MESSAGE

A faithful witness does not lie, but a false witness will utter lies.

Proverbs 14:5 NKJV

UNITY

When the enemy has caused division and dissention within my family, friendships, or community

If you have any encouragement from being united with Christ, if any comfort from His love, if any fellowship with the Spirit, if any tenderness and compassion, then make my joy complete by being like-minded, having the same love, being one in spirit and purpose. Do nothing out of selfish ambition or vain conceit, but in humility consider others better than yourselves. Each of you should look not only to your own interests, but also to the interests of others.

Philippians 2:1-4 NIV

Only let your conduct be worthy of the gospel of Christ, so that whether I come and see you or am absent, I may hear of your affairs, that you stand fast in one spirit, with one mind striving together for the faith of the gospel...

Philippians 1:27 NKJV

Just think - you don't need a thing, you've got it all! All God's gifts are right in front of you as you wait expectantly for our Master Jesus to arrive on the scene for the Finale. And not only that, but God Himself is right alongside to keep you steady and on track until things are all wrapped up by Jesus. God, who got you started in this spiritual adventure, shares with us the life of His Son and our Master Jesus. He will never give up on you. Never forget that. I have a serious concern to bring up with you, my friends, using the authority of Jesus, our Master. I'll put it as urgently as I can: you must along with each other. You must learn to be considerate of one another, cultivating a life in common.

1 Corinthians 1:7-10 THE MESSAGE

It was He who gave some to be apostles, some to be prophets, some to be evangelists, and some to be pastors and teachers, to prepare God's people for works of service, so that the body of Christ may be built up until we all reach unity in the faith and in the knowledge of the Son of God and become mature, attaining to the whole measure of the fullness of Christ. Then we will no longer be infants, tossed back and forth by the waves, and blown here and there by every wind of teaching and by the cunning and craftiness of men in their deceitful scheming. Instead, speaking the truth in love, we will in all things grow up into Him who is the Head, that is, Christ. From Him the whole body, joined and held together by every supporting ligament, grows and builds itself up in love, as each part does its work.

Ephesians 4:11-16 NIV

How good and pleasant it is when God's people live together in unity!

Psalm 133:1 NIV

But I have prayed for you, that your faith should not fail; and when you have returned to Me, strengthen your brethren.

Luke 22:32 NKJV

I in them and you in Me - so that they may be brought to complete unity. Then the world will know that You sent Me and have loved them even as You have loved Me.

John 17:23 NIV

Be kindly affectionate to one another with brotherly love, in honor giving preference to one another...

Romans 12:10 NKJV

We ought always to thank God for you, brothers, and rightly so, because your faith is growing more and more, and the love every one of you has for each other is increasing. Therefore, among God's churches we boast about your perseverance and faith in all the persecutions and trials you are enduring... God is just: He will pay back trouble to those who trouble you and give relief to you who are troubled, and to us as well.

2 Thessalonians 1:3-7 NIV

Make every effort to keep the unity of the Spirit through the bond of peace.

Ephesians 4:3 NIV

You, my brothers, were called to be free. But do not use your freedom to indulge the sinful nature, rather serve one another in love.

Galatians 5:13 NIV

Owe no one anything except to love one another, for he who loves another has fulfilled the law.

Romans 13:8 NKJV

Bear with each other and forgive one another if any of you has a grievance against someone. Forgive as the Lord forgave you. And over all these virtues put on love, which binds them all together in perfect unity. Let the peace of Christ rule in your hearts, since as members of one body you were called to peace. And be thankful.

Colossians 3:13-15 NIV

Finally, brethren, whatever things are true, whatever things are noble, whatever things are just, whatever things are pure, whatever things are lovely, whatever things are of good report, if there is any virtue and if there is anything praiseworthy - meditate on these things.

Philippians 4:8 NKJV

Finally, brethren, farewell. Become complete. Be of good comfort, be of one mind, live in peace; and the God of love and peace will be with you.

2 Corinthians 13:11 NKJV

Be completely humble and gentle; be patient, bearing with one another in love. Make every effort to keep the unity of the Spirit through the bond of peace. There is one body and one Spirit - just as you were called to one hope when you were called - one Lord, one faith, one baptism; one God and Father of all, Who is over all, and through all and in all.

Ephesians 4:2-6 NIV

Stand united, singular in vision, contending for people's trust in the Message, the Good News, not flinching or dodging in the slightest before the opposition. Your courage and unity will show them what they're up against: defeat for them, victory for you - and both because of God.

Philippians 1:27 THE MESSAGE

VICTORY

Because Jesus is my provider and protector, I am victorious in any situation

In famine, He'll keep you from starving. In war, from being hurt by the sword. You'll be protected from vicious gossip and live fearless through any catastrophe. You'll shrug off disaster and famine, and stroll fearlessly among wild animals. You'll be on good terms with rocks and mountains, wild animals will become your good friends. You'll know that your place on earth is safe. You'll look over your goods and find nothing amiss. You'll see your children grow up, your family lovely, and lissome as orchard grass. You'll arrive at your grave ripe with many good years, like sheaves of golden grain at harvest. Yes, this is the way things are – My word of honor. Take it to heart and you won't go wrong.

Job 5:20-27 THE MESSAGE

But you who held fast to the LORD your God are alive today, every one of you.

Deuteronomy 4:4 NKJV

'I create the fruit of the lips. Peace, peace to him who is far off, and to him who is near,' says the LORD, 'and I will

heal him, but the wicked are like the troubled sea, when it cannot rest, whose waters cast up mire and dirt. There is no peace for the wicked, says my God.'

Isaiah 57:19-21 NKJV

I have given you authority over all the power of the enemy, and you can walk among snakes and scorpions and crush them. Nothing will injure you.

Luke 10:19 NLT

But the Lord is faithful, who will establish you and guard you from the evil one. And we have confidence in the Lord concerning you both that you do and will do the things we command you.

2 Thessalonians 3:3-4 NKJV

'Because he loves me,' says the LORD, 'I will rescue him. I will protect him, for he acknowledges My Name. He will call upon Me, and I will answer him; I will be with him in trouble, I will deliver him and honor him. With long life will I satisfy him and show him My salvation.'

Psalm 91:14-16 NIV

Do not fear, for you will not be ashamed nor be disgraced...

Isaiah 54:4 NKJV

May the Lord answer you in the day of trouble! May the Name of the God of Jacob set you securely on high...may He grant you according to your heart's desire and fulfill all your plans. We will shout in triumph at your salvation and victory and in the name of our God, we will set up our banners. May the Lord fulfill all your petitions. Now I know that the Lord saves His anointed. He will answer him from His holy heaven with the saving strength of His right hand. Some trust in and boast of chariots and some of horses, but we will trust in and boast of the name of the Lord, our God...O Lord, give victory, let the King answer us when we call.

Psalm 20 AMP

I will love You, O LORD, my strength. The LORD is my rock and my fortress and my deliverer. My God, my strength, in Whom I will trust. My shield and the horn of my salvation, my stronghold. I will call upon the LORD who is worthy to be praised. So shall I be saved from my enemies.

Psalm 18:1-3 NKJV

Therefore, I will give thanks to You, O LORD... and sing praises to Your Name.

Psalm 18:46-49 NKJV

The LORD lives! Blessed be my Rock! Let the God of my salvation be exalted. It is God who avenges me, and subdues the people under me. He delivers me from my enemies. You also lift me up above those who rise against me. You have delivered me from the violent man.

Psalm 18:46-48 NKJV

To You, O LORD, I lift up my soul. O my God, I trust in You. Let me not be ashamed. Let not my enemies triumph over me. Indeed, let no one who waits on You be ashamed. Let those be ashamed who deal treacherously without cause.

Psalm 25:1-3 NKJV

Give us aid against the enemy, for the help of man is worthless. With God we will gain the victory, and He will trample down our enemies.

Psalm 60:11-12 NIV

Do not be deceived, God is not mocked; for whatever a man sows, that he will also reap.

Galatians 6:7 NKJV

Many seek the ruler's favor, but justice for man comes from the LORD.

Proverbs 29:26 NKJV

The LORD is good, a stronghold in the day of trouble; and He knows those who trust in Him.

Nahum 1:7 NKJV

For you shall not go out with haste, nor go by flight. For the LORD will go before you, and the God of Israel will be your rear guard.

Isaiah 52:12 NKJV

And that about wraps it up. God is strong, and He wants you strong. So take everything the Master has set out for you, well-made weapons of the best materials. And put them to use so you will be able to stand up to everything the devil throws your way. This is no afternoon athletic contest that we'll walk away from and forget about in a couple of hours. This is for keeps, a life-or- death fight to the finish against the devil and all his angels. Be prepared. You're up against far more than you can handle on your own. Take all the help you can get, every weapon God has issued, so that when it's all over but the shouting you'll still be on your feet. Truth, righteousness, peace, faith, and salvation are more than words. Learn how to apply them. You'll need them throughout your life. God's Word is an indispensable weapon. In the same way, prayer is essential in this ongoing warfare. Pray hard and long. Pray for your brothers and sisters. Keep your eyes open. Keep each other's spirits up so that no one falls behind or drops out.

Ephesians 6:10-18 THE MESSAGE

For the LORD your God is going with you! He will fight for you against your enemies, and he will give you victory!

Deuteronomy 20:4 NLT

'No weapon formed against you shall prosper; and every tongue which rises against you in judgment shall condemn. This is the heritage of the servants of the LORD, and their righteousness is from Me', says the LORD.

Isaiah 54:17 NKJV

A final word: Be strong in the Lord and in His mighty power. Put on all of God's armor so that you will be able to stand firm against all the strategies of the devil. For we are not fighting against flesh and blood enemies, but against evil rulers and authorities of the unseen world, against mighty powers in this dark world, and against evil spirits in the heavenly places. Therefore, put on every piece of God's armor so you will be able to resist the enemy in the time of evil. Then after the battle, you will be standing firm. Stand your ground, putting on the belt of truth and the body armor of God's righteousness. For shoes, put on the peace that comes from the Good News so that you will be fully prepared. In addition to all of these, hold up the shield of faith to stop the fiery arrows of the devil. Put on salvation as your helmet, and take the sword of the Spirit, which is the Word of God. Pray in the Spirit at all times and on every occasion. Stay alert and be persistent in your prayers for all believers everywhere.

Ephesians 6:10-18 NLT

The LORD is my light and my salvation - so why should I be afraid? The LORD is my fortress, protecting me from danger, so why should I tremble? When evil people come to devour me, when my enemies and foes attack me, they will stumble and fall. Though a mighty army surrounds me, my heart will not be afraid. Even if I am attacked, I will remain confident. The one thing I ask of the LORD - the thing I seek most, is to live in the house of the LORD all the days of my life, delighting in the LORD's perfections and meditating in His Temple. For He will conceal me there when troubles come; He will hide me in His sanctuary. He will place me out of reach on a high rock. Then I will hold my head high above my enemies who surround me. At His sanctuary I will offer sacrifices with shouts of joy, singing and praising the LORD with music. Hear me as I pray, O LORD. Be merciful and answer me! My heart has heard You say, 'Come and talk with Me.' And my heart responds, 'LORD, I am coming.' Do not turn Your back on me. Do not reject Your servant in anger. You have always been my Helper. Don't leave me now; don't abandon me, O God of my salvation! Even if my father and mother abandon me, the LORD will hold me close. Teach me how to live, O LORD. Lead me along the right path, for my enemies are waiting for me. Do not let me fall into their hands. For they accuse me of things I've never done; with every breath they threaten me with violence. Yet I am confident I will see the LORD's goodness while I am here in the land of the living. Wait patiently for the LORD. Be brave and courageous. Yes, wait patiently for the LORD.

Psalm 27 NLT

'Do not be afraid of them,' the LORD said to Joshua, 'for I have given you victory over them. Not a single one of them will be able to stand up to you.'

Joshua 10:8 NLT

Then Deborah said to Barak, 'Get ready! This is the day the LORD will give you victory over Sisera, for the LORD is marching ahead of you.'

Judges 4:14 NLT

For we were saved in this hope, but hope that is seen is not hope; for why does one still hope for what he sees? But if we hope for what we do not see, we eagerly wait for it with perseverance. Likewise the Spirit also helps in our weaknesses. For we do not know what we should pray for as we ought, but the Spirit Himself makes intercession for us with groanings which cannot be uttered. Now He who searches the hearts knows what the mind of the Spirit is, because He makes intercession for the saints according to the will of God. And we know that all things work together for good to those who love God, to those who are the called according to His purpose. For whom He foreknew, He also predestined to be conformed to the image of His Son, that He might be the firstborn among many brethren. Moreover whom He predestined, these He also called; whom He called, these He also justified; and whom He justified, these He also glorified. What then shall we say to these things? If God is for us, who can be against us? He who did not spare His own Son, but delivered Him up for us all, how shall He not with Him also freely give us all things? Who shall bring a charge against God's elect? It is God who justifies. Who is he who condemns? It is Christ who died, and furthermore is also risen, who is even at the right hand of God, who also makes intercession for us. Who shall separate us from the love of Christ? Shall tribulation, or distress, or persecution, or famine, or nakedness, or peril, or sword? As it is written: 'For Your sake we are killed all day long; We are accounted as sheep for the slaughter.' Yet in all these things we are more than conquerors through Him who loved us. For I am persuaded that neither death nor life, nor angels nor principalities nor powers, nor things present nor things to come, nor height nor depth, nor any other created thing, shall be able to separate us from the love of God which is in Christ Jesus our Lord.

Romans 8:24-39 NKJV

But God demonstrates His own love toward us, in that while we were still sinners, Christ died for us.

Romans 5:8 NKJV

From now on if you listen obediently to the commandments that I am commanding you today, love God, your God, and serve Him with everything you have within you, He'll take charge of sending the rain at the right time, both autumn and spring rains, so that you'll be able to harvest your grain, your grapes, your olives. He'll make sure there's plenty of grass for your animals. You'll have plenty to eat.

Deuteronomy 11:13-15 THE MESSAGE

For whatever is born of God overcomes the world. And this is the victory that has overcome the world – our faith.

1 John 5:4 NKJV

You stretched out Your right hand and the earth swallowed them up. But the people You redeemed, You led in merciful love; You guided them under Your protection to Your holy pasture.

Exodus 15:12 THE MESSAGE

Worship

To praise God for Who He is and for all He has done

I will mention the loving kindnesses of the LORD and the praises of the LORD. According to all that the LORD has bestowed on us and the great goodness toward the house of Israel, which He has bestowed on them according to His loving kindnesses.

Isaiah 63:7 NKJV

It's who you are and the way you live that count before God. Your worship must engage your spirit in the pursuit of truth. That's the kind of people the Father is out looking for: those who are simply and honestly themselves before Him in their worship. God is sheer being itself - Spirit. Those who worship Him must do it out of their very being, their spirits, their true selves, in adoration.

John 4:23 THE MESSAGE

The LORD is my strength and my defense; He has become my salvation. He is my God, and I will praise Him, my father's God, and I will exalt Him.

Exodus 15:2 NIV

I will praise the LORD according to His righteousness, and will sing praise to the name of the LORD Most High.

Psalm 7:17 NKJV

When my life was slipping away, I remembered God, and my prayer got through to You, made it all the way to Your Holy Temple. Those who worship hollow gods, god-frauds, walk away from their only true love. But I'm worshiping You, God, calling out in thanksgiving!

Jonah 2:1 THE MESSAGE

Sing praise-songs to God. He's done it all! Let the whole earth know what he's done! Raise the roof!

Isaiah 12:25 THE MESSAGE

Mighty God! Far beyond our reach! Unsurpassable in power and justice! It's unthinkable that He'd treat anyone unfairly. So bow to Him in deep reverence, one and all! If you're wise, you'll most certainly worship Him.

Job 37: 23 THE MESSAGE

Praise the LORD, for He has shown me the wonders of His unfailing love.

Psalm 31:21 NLT

He is the one you praise; He is your God, who performed for you those great and awesome wonders you saw with your own eyes.

Deuteronomy 10:21 NIV

Look! Striding across the mountains - a messenger bringing the latest good news: peace! A holiday, Judah! Celebrate! Worship and recommit to God! No more worries about this enemy. This one is history. Close the books.

Nahum 1:15 THE MESSAGE

O LORD God, You have begun to show Your servant, Your greatness and Your mighty hand, for what god is there in heaven or on earth who can do anything like Your works and Your might deeds?

Deuteronomy 3:24 NKJV

David said to Abigail, 'Praise be to the LORD, the God of Israel, who has sent you today to meet me.'

1 Samuel 25:32 NIV

Worship the Lord your God, and only Him. Serve Him with absolute single- heartedness.

Matthew 4:10 THE MESSAGE

When I consider Your heavens, the work of Your fingers, the moon and the stars, which You have ordained, what is man that You are mindful of him? And the son of man that You visit him? For You have made him a little lower than the angels, and You have crowned him with glory and honor...O LORD, our LORD, how excellent is Your Name in all the earth!

Psalm 8:3-5, 9 NKJV

I will praise You, O LORD, with my whole heart. I will tell of all Your marvelous works. I will be glad and rejoice in You. I will sing praise to Your name, O Most High. When my enemies turn back, they shall fall and perish at Your presence. For You have maintained my right and my cause. You sat on the throne judging in righteousness. You have rebuked the nations. You have destroyed the wicked.

Psalm 9:1-5 NKJV

Make sure you don't take things for granted and go slack in working for the common good; share what you have with others. God takes particular pleasure in acts of worship - a different kind of 'sacrifice' - that take place in kitchen and workplace and on the streets.

Hebrews 13:16 THE MESSAGE

GOD is about to bring you into a good land, a land with brooks and rivers, springs and lakes, streams out of the hills and through the valleys. It's a land of wheat and barley, of vines and figs and pomegranates, of olives, oil, and honey. It's land where you'll never go hungry - always food on the table and a roof over your head. It's a land where you'll get iron out of rocks and mine copper from the hills. After a meal, satisfied, bless GOD, your God, for the good land He has given you. Make sure you don't forget GOD, your God, by not keeping His commandments, His rules and regulations that I command you today. Make sure that when you eat and are satisfied, build pleasant houses and settle in, see your herds and flocks flourish and more and more money come in, watch your standard of living going up and up - make sure you don't become so full of yourself and your things that you forget GOD, your God, the God who delivered you from Egyptian slavery; the God who led you through that huge and fearsome wilderness, those desolate, arid badlands crawling with fiery snakes and scorpions; the God who gave you water gushing from hard rock; the God who gave you manna to eat in the wilderness, something your ancestors had never heard of, in order to give you a taste of the hard life, to test you so that you would be prepared to live well in the days ahead of you.

Deuteronomy 8:1-16 THE MESSAGE

Do you see what we've got? An unshakable kingdom! And do you see how thankful we must be? Not only thankful, but brimming with worship, deeply reverent before God.

Hebrews 12:28 THE MESSAGE

Sing to God a brand-new song, sing His praises all over the world! Let the sea and its fish give a round of applause, with all the far-flung islands joining in. Let the desert and its camps raise a tune, calling the Kedar nomads to join in. Let the villagers in Sela round up a choir and perform from the tops of the mountains. Make God's glory resound; echo His praises from coast to coast.

Isaiah 42:10 THE MESSAGE

Give praise to the LORD, proclaim His Name; make known among the nations what He has done.

1 Chronicles 16:8 NIV

Your eyes are windows into your body. If you open your eyes wide in wonder and belief, your body fills up with light. If you live squinty-eyed in greed and distrust, your body is a dank cellar. If you pull the blinds on your windows, what a dark life you will have! You can't worship two gods at once. Loving one god, you'll end up hating the other. Adoration of one feeds contempt for the other. You can't worship God and Money both. If you decide for God, living a life of God-worship, it follows that you don't fuss about what's on the table at mealtimes or whether the clothes in your closet are in fashion. There is far more to your life than the food you put in your stomach, more to your outer appearance than the clothes you hang on your body. Look at the birds, free and unfettered, not tied down to a job description, careless in the care of God. And you count far more to Him than birds.

Matthew 6:22-26 THE MESSAGE

All who were standing around the throne — Angels, Elders, Animals — fell on their faces before the throne and worshiped God, singing: Oh, Yes! The blessing and glory and wisdom and thanksgiving, the honor and power and strength, to our God forever and ever and ever! Oh, Yes!

Revelation 7:9 THE MESSAGE

The LORD lives! Praise be to my Rock! Exalted be my God, the Rock, my Savior!

2 Samuel 22:47 NIV

The woman to be admired and praised is the woman who lives in the [reverence] of God. Give her everything she deserves! Festoon her life with praises!

Proverbs 31: 11 THE MESSAGE

But let all who take refuge in you rejoice; let them sing joyful praises forever. Spread your protection over them, that all who love your name may be filled with joy.

Psalm 5:11 NLT

When you have eaten your fill, be sure to praise the LORD your God for the good land he has given you.

Deuteronomy 8:10 NLT

Praise the LORD who has given rest to His people Israel, just as He promised. Not one word has failed of all the wonderful promises He gave through His servant Moses.

1 Kings 8:56 NLT

I will declare Your Name to my brethren...and sing praise to You.

Hebrews 2:12 NKJV

I shall not die, but live, and declare the works of the LORD.

Psalm 118:17 NKJV

"X"

For any variable that life throws at me

Who shall separate us from the love of Christ? Shall tribulation, or distress, or persecution, or famine, or nakedness, or peril, or sword?... Yet in all these things we are more than conquerors through Him who loved us. For I am persuaded that neither death nor life, nor angels nor principalities nor powers, nor things present nor things to come, nor height nor depth, nor any other created thing, shall be able to separate us from the love of God which is in Christ Jesus our Lord.

Romans 8:35, 37-39 NKJV

I will instruct you and teach you in the way you should go; I will guide you with My eye.

Psalm 32:8 NKJV

Let not your heart be troubled; you believe in God, believe also in Me.

John 14:1 NKJV

I am always with You; You hold me by my right hand. You guide me with Your counsel and afterward, You will take me into glory.

Psalm 73:23-24 NIV

Why are you cast down, O my soul? And why are you disquieted within me? Hope in God; For I shall yet praise Him, the help of my countenance and my God.

Psalm 43:5 NKJV

Trust God from the bottom of your heart; don't try to figure out everything on your own. Listen for God's voice in everything you do, everywhere you go; He's the one who will keep you on track. Don't assume that you know it all. Run to God! Run from evil! Your body will glow with health, your very bones will vibrate with life! Honor God with everything you own; give Him the first and the best. Your barns will burst, your wine vats will brim over. But don't, dear friend, resent God's discipline; don't sulk under His loving correction. It's the child He loves that God corrects; a father's delight is behind all this.

Proverbs 3:5-12 THE MESSAGE

Blessed is the man who trusts in the LORD, and whose hope is the LORD. For he shall be like a tree planted by the waters which spreads out its roots by the river, and will not fear when heat comes, but its leaf will be green and will not be anxious in the year of drought, nor will cease from yielding fruit.

Jeremiah 17:7-8 NKJV

Here's what I want you to do: Find a quiet, secluded place so you won't be tempted to role- play before God. Just be there as simply and honestly as you can manage. The focus will shift from you to God, and you will begin to sense His grace.

Matthew 6:6 THE MESSAGE

Now if God so clothes the grass of the field, which today is, and tomorrow is thrown into the oven, will He not much more clothe you, O you of little faith?

Matthew 6:30 NKJV

But He said to them, 'Why are you fearful, O you of little faith?' Then He arose and rebuked the winds and the sea, and there was a great calm.

Matthew 8:26 NKJV

Friends, when life gets really difficult, don't jump to the conclusion that God isn't on the job. Instead, be glad that you are in the very thick of what Christ experienced. This is a spiritual refining process, with glory just around the corner.

1 Peter 4:12-13 THE MESSAGE

Cast your burden on the LORD and He shall sustain you; He shall never permit the righteous to be moved.

Psalm 55:22 NKJV

Don't worry about the wicked or envy those who do wrong. For like grass, they soon fade away. Like spring flowers, they soon wither. Trust in the LORD and do good. Then you will live safely in the land and prosper. Take delight in the LORD, and He will give you your heart's desires. Commit everything you do to the LORD. Trust Him, and He will help you. He will make your innocence radiate like the dawn, and the justice of your cause will shine like the noonday sun. Be still in the presence of the LORD, and wait patiently for Him to act. Don't worry about evil people who prosper or fret about their wicked schemes. Stop being angry! Turn from your rage! Do not lose your temper - it only leads to harm. For the wicked will be destroyed, but those who trust in the LORD will possess the land. Soon the wicked will disappear. Though you look for them, they will be gone. The lowly will possess the land and will live in peace and prosperity. The wicked plot against the Godly; they snarl at them in defiance. But the LORD just laughs, for He sees their day of judgment coming. The wicked draw their swords and string their bows to kill the poor and the oppressed, to slaughter those who do right. But their swords will stab their own hearts, and their bows will be broken. It is better to be Godly and have little than to be evil and rich. For the strength of the wicked will be shattered, but the LORD takes care of the Godly. Day by day the LORD takes care of the innocent, and they will receive an inheritance that lasts forever. They will not be disgraced in hard times; even in famine they will have more than enough. But the wicked will die. The LORD's enemies are like flowers in a field - they will disappear like smoke. The wicked borrow and never repay, but the Godly are generous givers. Those the LORD blesses will possess the land, but those He curses will die. The LORD directs the steps of the Godly. He delights in every detail of their lives. Though they stumble, they will never fall, for the LORD holds them by the hand. Once I was young, and now I am old. Yet I have never seen the Godly abandoned or their children begging for bread. The Godly always give generous loans to others, and their children are a blessing. Turn from evil and do good, and you will live in the land forever. For the LORD loves justice, and He will never abandon the Godly. He will keep them safe forever, but the children of the wicked will die. The Godly will possess the land and will live there forever. The Godly offer good counsel; they teach right from wrong. They have made God's law their own, so they will never slip from His path. The wicked wait in ambush for the Godly, looking for an excuse to kill them. But the LORD will not let the wicked succeed or let the Godly be condemned when they are put on trial. Put your hope in the LORD. Travel steadily along His path. He will honor you by giving you the land. You will see the wicked destroyed. I have seen wicked and ruthless people flourishing like a tree in its native soil. But when I looked again, they were gone! Though I searched for them, I could not find them! Look at those who are honest and good, for a wonderful future awaits those who love peace. But the rebellious will be destroyed; they have no future. The LORD rescues the Godly; He is their fortress in times of trouble. The LORD helps them, rescuing them from the wicked. He saves them, and they find shelter in Him.

Psalm 37 NLT

Take My yoke upon you. Let Me teach you, because I am humble and gentle at heart, and you will find rest for your souls.

Matthew 11:29 NLT

No temptation has overtaken you except such as is common to man; but God is faithful, Who will not allow you to be tempted beyond what you are able, but with the temptation will also make the way of escape, that you may be able to bear it.

1 Corinthians 10:13 NKJV

For I am confident of this very thing that He who began a good work in you will perfect it until the day of Christ Jesus.

Philippians 1:6 NASB

'I will visit you and perform My good work towards you, and cause you to return to this place. For I know the thoughts that I think towards you,' says the LORD, 'thoughts of peace and not of evil, to give you a future and a hope. Then you will call upon Me and go and pray to Me, and I will listen to you. And you will seek Me and find Me, when you search for Me with all your heart. I will be found by you,' says the LORD, 'and I will bring you back from your captivity.'

Jeremiah 29:11-14 NIV

Be anxious for nothing, but in everything by prayer and supplication, with thanksgiving, let your requests be made known to God; and the peace of God, which surpasses all understanding, will guard your hearts and minds through Christ Jesus.

Philippians 4:6-7 NKJV

I will lift up my eyes to the hills - from whence comes my help? My help comes from the LORD, Who made heaven and earth. He will not allow your foot to be moved; He who keeps you will not slumber. Behold, He who keeps Israel shall neither slumber nor sleep. The LORD is your keeper; the LORD is your shade at your right hand. The sun shall not strike you by day, nor the moon by night. The LORD shall preserve you from all evil; He shall preserve your soul. The LORD shall preserve your going out and your coming in from this time forth, and even forevermore.

Psalm 121 NKJV

YIELDING

To surrender and trust in God's better plan for me instead

Now may the Lord direct your hearts into the love of God and into the patience of Christ.

2 Thessalonians 3:5 NKJV

The heart is hopelessly dark and deceitful, a puzzle that no one can figure out. But I, God, search the heart and examine the mind. I get to the heart of the human. I get to the root of things. I treat them as they really are and not as they pretend to be.

Jeremiah 17:9-10 THE MESSAGE

No temptation has overtaken you except such as is common to man; but God is faithful, who will not allow you to be tempted beyond what you are able, but with the temptation will also make a way of escape, that you may be able to bear it.

1 Corinthians10:13 NKJV

For in that He Himself has suffered, being tempted, He is able to aid those who are tempted.

Hebrews 2:18 NKJV

Therefore, submit to God. Resist the devil and he will flee from you.

James 4:7 NKJV

So they answered Joshua saying, 'All that you command us we will do, and wherever you send us, we will go. Just as we heeded Moses in all things, so we will heed you...'

Joshua 1:16-17 NKJV

With God all things are possible.

Matthew 19:26 NKJV

Surrender your heart to God, turn to Him in prayer...

Job 11:13 THE MESSAGE

Test all things; hold fast what is good. Abstain from every form of evil.

1 Thessalonians 5:21-2 NKJV

You test the heart and have pleasure in uprightness.

1 Chronicles 29:17 NKJV

I AM the true grapevine, and My Father is the gardener. He cuts off every branch of Mine that doesn't produce fruit, and He prunes the branches that do bear fruit so they will produce even more. You have already been pruned and purified by the message I have given you. Remain in Me, and I will remain in you. For a branch cannot produce fruit if it is severed from the vine, and you cannot be fruitful unless you remain in Me. Yes, I am the vine; you are the branches. Those who remain in Me, and I in them, will produce much fruit. For apart from Me you can do nothing. Anyone who does not remain in Me is thrown away like a useless branch and withers. Such branches are gathered into a pile to be burned. But if you remain in Me and my words remain in you, you may ask for anything you want, and it will be granted! When you produce much fruit, you are My true disciples. This brings great glory to My Father. I have loved you even as the Father has loved Me. Remain in My love. When you obey My commandments, you remain in My love, just as I obey My Father's commandments and remain in His love. I have told you these things so that you will be filled with My joy. Yes, your joy will overflow! This is My commandment: Love each other in the same way I have loved you. There is no greater love than to lay down one's life for one's friends. You are My friends if you do what I command. I no longer call you slaves, because a master doesn't confide in his slaves. Now you are My friends, since I have told you everything the Father told Me. You didn't choose Me. I chose you. I appointed you to go and produce lasting fruit, so that the Father will give you whatever you ask for, using My Name. This is My command: Love each other.

John 15:1-17 NLT

For this is the love of God, that we keep His commandments. And His commandments are not burdensome. For whatever is born of God overcomes the world. And this is the victory that has overcome the world – our faith.

1 John 5:3-4 NKJV

Put on the Lord Jesus Christ, and make no provision for the flesh to fulfill its lusts.

Romans 13:14 NKJV

But I discipline my body and bring it into subjection, lest, when I have preached to others, I myself should become disqualified.

1 Corinthians 9:27 NKJV

Patience can persuade a prince, and soft speech can crush opposition.

Proverbs 25:15 NLT

Bring the whole tithe into the storehouse that there may be food in My house. 'Test Me on this', says the LORD Almighty, 'and see if I will not throw open the floodgates of heaven and pour out so much blessing that you will not have room enough for it.'

Malachi 3:10 NIV

Now may the God of peace Himself sanctify you completely, and may your whole spirit, soul and body be preserved blameless at the coming of our Lord Jesus Christ. He who calls you is faithful, who also will do it.

1 Thessalonians 5:23-24 NKJV

Now the purpose of the commandment is love from a pure heart, from a good conscience, and from sincere faith.

1 Timothy 1:5 NKJV

For though we live in the world, we do not wage war as the world does. The weapons we fight with are not the weapons of the world. On the contrary, they have divine power to demolish strongholds. We demolish arguments and every pretension that sets itself up against the knowledge of God, and we take captive every thought to make it obedient to Christ.

2 Corinthians 10:3-5 NIV

Surrender to God All-Powerful! You will find peace and prosperity

Job 22:21 THE MESSAGE

ZEALOUSNESS

To glorify God by living a purposeful life, as I joyfully contribute to others

Oh, taste and see that the LORD is good. Blessed is the man who trusts in Him! Oh, have reverence for the LORD, you His saints! There is no want to those who fear Him...but those who seek the LORD shall not lack any good thing.

Psalm 34:8-10 NKJV

Rejoice always, pray without ceasing, in everything give thanks; for this is the will of God in Christ Jesus for you.

1 Thessalonians 5:16-18 NKJV

Pursue a righteous life - a life of wonder, faith, love, steadiness, courtesy. Run hard and fast in the faith. Seize the eternal life, the life you were called to, the life you so fervently embraced in the presence of so many witnesses.

1 Timothy 6:11 THE MESSAGE

Blessed are You, LORD God of Israel, our Father, forever and ever. Yours, O LORD, is the greatness, the power and the glory, the victory and the majesty; for all that is in heaven and in earth is Yours. Yours is the kingdom, O LORD, and You are exalted as head over all. Both riches and honor come from You, and You reign over all. In Your hand is power and might. In Your hand it is to make great and to give strength to all. Now therefore, our God, we thank You and praise Your glorious name. But who am I, and who are my people that we should be able to offer so willingly as this? For all things come from You, and of Your own we have given You. For we are aliens and pilgrims before You, as were all our fathers...

1 Chronicles 29:10-15 NKJV

They pleaded with Samuel, 'Pray with all your might! And don't let up! Pray to GOD, our GOD, that He'll save us from the boot of the Philistines.' Samuel...prayed fervently to GOD, interceding for Israel. And GOD answered.

1 Samuel 7:8-9 THE MESSAGE

Praise the LORD, O my soul, all my inmost being, praise His Holy Name. Praise the LORD, O my soul, and forget not all His benefits – Who forgives all your sins and heals all your diseases, Who redeems your life from the pit and crowns you with love and compassion, Who satisfies your desires with good things so that your youth is renewed like the eagle's.

Psalm 103:1-5 NIV

Praise the LORD! I will praise the LORD with my whole heart...the works of the LORD are great, studied by all who have pleasure in them. His work is honorable and glorious and His righteousness endures forever. He has made His wonderful works to be remembered; the LORD is gracious and full of compassion. He has given food to those who fear Him. He will ever be mindful of His covenant. He has declared to His people the power of His works, in giving them the heritage of the nations. The works of His hands are verity and justice; all His precepts are sure. They stand fast forever and ever, and are done in truth and uprightness. He has sent redemption to His people. He has commanded His covenant forever. Holy and awesome is His Name. The fear and reverence of the LORD is the beginning of wisdom; a good understanding have all those who do His commandments. His praise endures forever.

Psalm 111 NIV

God doesn't come and go. God lasts. He is Creator of all you can see or imagine. He doesn't get tired out, doesn't pause to catch His breath, and He knows everything, inside and out. He energizes those who get tired, gives fresh strength to dropouts. For even young people tire and drop out, young folk in their prime stumble and fall. But those who wait upon God get fresh strength. They spread their wings and soar like eagles. They run and don't get tired, they walk and don't lag behind.

Isaiah 40:28-31 NIV

The heavens proclaim the glory of God. The skies display His craftsmanship. Day after day they continue to speak; night after night they make Him known. They speak without a sound or word; their voice is never heard, yet their message has gone throughout the earth, and their words to all the world. God has made a home in the heavens for the sun. It bursts forth like a radiant bridegroom after his wedding. It rejoices like a great athlete eager to run the race. The sun rises at one end of the heavens and follows its course to the other end. Nothing can hide from its heat. The instructions of the LORD are perfect, reviving the soul. The decrees of the LORD are trustworthy, making wise the simple. The commandments of the LORD are right, bringing joy to the heart. The commands of the LORD are clear, giving insight for living. Reverence for the LORD is pure, lasting forever. The laws of the LORD are true; each one is fair. They are more desirable than gold, even the finest gold. They are sweeter than honey, even honey dripping from the comb. They are a warning to your servant, a great reward for those who obey them. How can I know all the sins lurking in my heart? Cleanse me from these hidden faults. Keep your servant from deliberate sins! Don't let them control me. Then I will be free of guilt and innocent of great sin. May the words of my mouth and the meditation of my heart be pleasing to you, O LORD, my rock and my redeemer.

Psalm 19 NLT

I will praise the Name of God with a song, and will magnify Him with thanksgiving.

Psalm 69:30 NKJV

No man shall be able to stand before you all the days of your life; as I was with Moses, so I will be with you. I will not leave you nor forsake you. Be strong and of good courage, for to this people you shall divide as an inheritance the land, which I swore to their fathers to give them. Only be strong and very courageous, that you may observe to do according to all the law which Moses My servant commanded you; do not turn from it to the right hand or to the left, that you may prosper wherever you go. This Book of the Law shall not depart from your mouth, but you shall meditate in it day and night, that you may observe to do according to all that is written in it. For then you will make your way prosperous, and then you will have good success. Have I not commanded you? Be strong and of good courage; do not be afraid, nor be dismayed, for the LORD your God is with you wherever you go.

Joshua 1:5-9 NKJV

Who may worship in Your sanctuary, LORD? Who may enter Your presence on Your holy hill? Those who lead blameless lives and do what is right, speaking the Truth from sincere hearts. Those who refuse to gossip or harm their neighbors or speak evil of their friends. Those who despise flagrant sinners, and honor the faithful followers of the LORD, and keep their promises, even when it hurts... such people will stand firm forever.

Psalm 15 NLT

Praise the LORD! Oh, give thanks to the LORD, for He is good! For His mercy endures forever.

Psalm 106:1 NKJV

We have different gifts, according to the grace given to each of us. If your gift is prophesying, then prophesy in accordance with your faith; if it is serving, then serve; if it is teaching, then teach; if it is to encourage, then give encouragement; if it is giving, then give generously; if it is to lead, do it diligently; if it is to show mercy, do it cheerfully. Love must be sincere. Hate what is evil; cling to what is good. Be devoted to one another in love. Honor one another above yourselves. Never be lacking in zeal, but keep your spiritual fervor, serving the LORD. Be joyful in hope, patient in affliction, faithful in prayer. Share with the LORD's people who are in need. Practice hospitality. Bless those who persecute you; bless and do not curse. Rejoice with those who rejoice; mourn with those who mourn. Live in harmony with one another. Do not be proud, but be willing to associate with people of low position. Do not be conceited. Do not repay anyone evil for evil. Be careful to do what is right in the eyes of everyone. If it is possible, as far as it depends on you, live at peace with everyone. Do not take revenge, my dear friends, but leave room for God's wrath, for it is written: 'It is Mine to avenge; I will repay,' says the LORD.

Romans 12:6-20 NIV

Oh, that men would give thanks to the LORD for His goodness, and for His wonderful works to the children of men!

Psalm 107:8 NKJV

Among the gods there is none like You, O LORD; Nor are there any works like Your works. All nations whom You have made shall come and worship before You, O LORD, and shall glorify Your Name for You are great and do wondrous things. You alone are God. Teach me Your way, O LORD; I will walk in Your truth. Unite my heart to fear Your Name. I will praise You, O LORD my God, with all my heart and I will glorify Your Name forevermore.

Psalm 86:8-12 NKJV

DEAR FRIEND,

I hope that these excerpts from God's Love Letters have blessed you and given you new insights to His beautiful, kind, gentle, patient, and amazing nature.

No matter what is going on around you, no matter what situations are before you, just reflect on His promises shared in this book. Remember that...

His mercies are not only tender and abundant, but they are new every morning. He is your high tower. Run to Him and He will protect you, keep you safe, and give you strength. His thoughts and plans are for you—to have a bright and exceedingly abundant future. He wants to give you hope, peace, joy, blessings; he wants you not to suffer evil.

Be assured that God, Who began a good work in you, will be faithful to complete it because His faithfulness endures forever! It never ceases! Even if you feel like quitting, or if you have little faith, God will never give up on you, nor will He leave you. In fact, He will carry you through each and every storm.

God has His angels encamped around you and they will defend you. No weapon formed against you shall prosper. God has not given you a spirit of fear but of power, love and a sound mind. So take comfort in Him, knowing that He walks with you in the shadows, and He will never, ever, e-v-e-r leave you or forsake you.

He loves you from everlasting to everlasting—it's limitless, changeless—and it's real love because He is real. All your mistakes and inadequacies are cast into the sea and are forgotten as far as the east is to the west, never to be seen or remembered again. If you seek Him with all your heart and strength, He will be found. Even if you are in the pit of hell, He is there with you, and if you soar into the sky, He is there, too. Just seek Him. God will make your crooked paths straight and He will be a lamp unto your feet. He will share the secrets of the universe with you. All you need to do is to seek Him and ask.

God will renew your strength and you will not grow weary, nor be faint. Instead, you will soar as if you had the wings of an eagle and He will work ALL THINGS TOGETHER for good. He loves you so much that He has every tear of yours in a bottle. He counts AND names every single hair on your head, thinking about you more in one moment of time than there are grains of sands on the whole earth.

Yes, there may be times when you feel lonely, but know that nothing will ever separate you from God's love—neither life nor death, angels nor demons, fears for today nor worries about tomorrow—NOTHING will ever separate you from His love.

Even if hundreds of thousands of people are against you, since God is with you and for you, you have the majority, and you are victorious. You fight from victory, not for victory!

In Christ, you have already won!

So, do not be afraid, for He is with you. Only a fool would dare be against you! Do not be dismayed for THE GOD of the universe is with you to help you, strengthen you, defend you, uphold you, fight for you, restore you, and renew you. God has redeemed you and will bless you for eternity because He not only called you, He chose you to be His, and His alone, forever.

God's Name is Faithful and True, the Great Provider, the Great Physician, and The Lord of Hosts. Yet, He is also your Papa, your Redeemer and your Prince of Peace.

Yes, there will be times when He, in His pure love and mighty wisdom, will allow trials to come, but they will be used to strengthen, empower and equip you, while humbling and training your heart, mind and spirit at the same time. This is so you can be genuinely strong, sincerely loving of others, and properly prepared and not in harm's way as you step out into your calling.

All He asks is that you trust Him. He has never let you down, and He will never, ever let you down. You may not understand why certain things or situations are the way they are. But His ways are not your ways. His thoughts are not your thoughts. He is LORD GOD and He is at work, making sure ALL THINGS TOGETHER are for your good! Just trust Him.

If you're in a storm, don't give up hope! You're going to the other side! The story is not over yet! You are only in a small chapter of the most amazing story ever told! Just be strong and very courageous. He will carry you through to the other side! Be at peace and be comforted. God calls you His friend—and He is a good and faithful friend! Be happy and rejoice! You are friends with Someone beyond description in any language! He is marvelous, magnificent and awesome! Seriously, THE GOD of the universe is your friend!

Think about that!

THE GOD of the universe, who flung the stars into the sky with His fingertips and breathed the galaxies into existence, loves you, died for you, fights for you every day, and wants to be your friend! THE GOD of the universe sets His eyes on you! He longs to spend time with you. He wants you to trust Him, and to share a loyal and loving friendship with Him. Will you trust Him? Will you love Him back?

Do you get how BIG this is?!

All He asks is for you to 'just believe.' And when you do, you will make His heart leap for joy! And you will live a life that is unimaginable—beyond your most outrageous dreams. No eye has seen, nor ear has heard, nor any human mind can conceive what God has prepared for those who love Him.

Just believe.

God loves you so much and has waited thousands and thousands of years for this day—the day you are reading a few of His love letters to you through this book.

There is much, much more to share, but I hope that for now these Words will be tender yet powerful reminders of who you are, how brilliant you are, and how loved you are!

Take your time contemplating each passage. Open your heart and allow God's Spirit to touch you through His Word. Before you know it, you will be experiencing the peace, joy, hope, strength, and love that truly surpasses all understanding.

It's no accident that you are reading this book at this time.

God knew that His Words would one day reach you, touch you, comfort you, and encourage you... "for such a time as this".

Life will always have its ups and downs, but it's better to go through the storms with God by your side, than to face those storms without Him.

Remember, He is always with you. He will never, ever, ever forsake you, and He will always go before you—just follow His footsteps.

Only believe!

Now, may…

The LORD bless you and keep you. The LORD make His face shine upon you, and be gracious to you. The LORD lift up His countenance upon you, and give you peace.

Numbers 6:24-26 NKJV

In joyful, loving service,

Manna Ko

San Diego, California, 2014

AN INVITATION

The world's answers to pain and suffering are temporary at best. Go to God with your cares instead and claim your victory in every circumstance with Him.

Accepting Jesus Christ as your LORD and Savior is your choice, and it requires your heartfelt awareness and sincerity. If you've never asked God into your life before (or if you have in the past, but have drifted away and want to renew your relationship) will you take a chance and believe in Him, and ask Him into your life, right now?

Yes, God does love you, more than you will ever know, and He's knocking now at the door of your heart. Will you let Him in? It's as simple as saying, "Yes. I believe."

This will be one of the most brilliant and amazing choices of your life. It's simple. Turn the page, read the prayer from your heart...

And simply, believe.

Dear God,

I am tired and weary.

I don't know what else to do, or where else to go. I don't want to keep doing everything alone or on my own strength. It's difficult to trust in things or in people, but I am willing to trust in You.

Please forgive me for all my wrongdoings, known and unknown to my conscious mind. I often live by habit and am not always aware of, nor am open to, all my mistakes, shortcomings, weaknesses, or faults. It's been much easier to blame others—and You—so I didn't have to take responsibility for my life.

The consequences of this way of living are painful, and what I've settled for is no longer acceptable. I want to change my ways and am ready to do so with You.

I need You, and I believe in You. I believe in Your Son, Jesus Christ, and I believe that because You love me more than I can ever imagine or comprehend, You sent Your precious Son, Jesus Christ, to save me by dying on the Cross to pay for my sins. I believe that He rose from the grave, is alive reigning by Your side, and because He exchanged His Life for my own, I am now saved, redeemed, and can be with You forever.

Because of Jesus, I am a slave to no one. I am free in You. Please show me how to live a full and meaningful life. Help me to be more like You in how I think, in what I say, and in what I do. Soften my heart so I can really know You and be more like You.

I eagerly dedicate my life to You now. Protect me and guide me. Live in me now, and be with me forever.

Thank You, God.

In Jesus Christ's Holy Name, I pray. Amen.

If you just prayed this prayer, then welcome to the family! God wants to share a great life together with you! Find a Bible-teaching church that celebrates the fullness of God, and get ready to have your socks blown off by a life filled with true love, miracles, purpose, and exceedingly abundant joy!

ACKNOWLEDGEMENTS

I have been working on this book for 12 years, and after what seems like countless revisions to format, style and approach, at long last it is ready to be your "Spiritual First Aid Kit", your immediate go-to resource when you need more than just a band aid approach to what is going on in your life.

This project would never have become a reality were it not for the unfaltering love and support of some very special people in my life. I am very grateful for my beloved family whose steadfast love lifts me up daily; for my faithful friends who cheer me on in every endeavor; and mostly, I want to thank my Best Friend, Jesus Christ, Who spoke these Words to me through each tear and smile, and in each failure and triumph.

And now, to my new friends, this book is not meant to be an exhaustive resource, but rather a humble sampling of inspirational Truths that can bring immediate relief to your situation. May every letter of every word in this book bring you encouragement, comfort, boldness, wisdom, peace, hope, and joy as you victoriously step into each circumstance with God.

Blessings upon blessings to you.

ABOUT MANNA

Manna began her career as an entrepreneur in the 1980s in Canada, and within a very short time, became nationally recognized for her work. In the late 1990s she and her son moved to the United States, where she used her giftings and expertise to help others in the marketplace, providing progressive marketing concepts, effective office systems, integrative team building curricula, and personal and professional leadership consulting.

After a life-altering event in the early 2000s, Manna went back to school to learn as much as she could about "life" to understand the deeper dynamics in relationships, health and healing. With herself as living proof of miracles happening to everyday people, she earned an MA in Psychology, a PhD in Philosophy, and additional certifications as a Holistic Health Practitioner (HHP), a Certified Clinical Nutritionist (CCN), and a Certified Clinical Herbalist (CCH), among many others. Upon completion of her studies, she opened up her own wellness center to help others.

As an Author, Speaker, Leader, Visionary, CEO and Founder of several companies, and Strategic Partner to many others, Manna is passionate about helping people step into their calling, live extraordinary lives, prosper through chaos, be a forerunner with unseen opportunities, lead under pressure, and deliver results.

Manna's own calling is to teach, stretch, and equip others to live-out their gifts and destiny in a world hungry for authentic, honorable, and meaningful leadership and relationships. Conventional models teach us to seek more information; Manna teaches us to develop wisdom. In this way, not only will the individual prosper, but the entire community will prosper.

Now with over twenty-seven years of entrepreneurial experience, she has spoken to over 40,000 people, worked with hundreds of different businesses and organizations, and guided even more individuals seeking personal excellence. She has clients in 8 countries, has contributed to numerous educational, disciplinary and advisory boards, and is an Ordained Leader with Third Day Churches. She is also a marathon runner, a health and exercise enthusiast, an avid reader, is conversant in four languages, plays tennis and the piano, studied martial arts, and is active in her community. Returning recently from an extended sabbatical where Manna served on mission trips, she also took quiet time to dive into her writing again. While she had already written numerous books, articles, curricula, manuals and programs in the past, her writing now has extended to deeper levels as she shares her own fascinating life's journey in her recently published autobiographical novel, *Made For More*.

Manna's background is all at once unusual, unimaginable, diverse, extensive, and rich. She has overcome great adversities, and is living proof that having - and living, "happily ever after" is possible, even against all odds.

Manna and her family live in San Diego, California.

My face is set, my gait is fast, my goal is Heaven, my road is narrow, my way is rough, my companions are few, my Guide is reliable, my mission is clear. I cannot be bought, compromised, detoured, lured away, turned back, diluted, or delayed. I will not flinch in the face of sacrifice, hesitate in the presence of adversity, negotiate at the table of the enemy, ponder at the pool of popularity, or meander in a maze of mediocrity. I won't give up, shut up, let up, or slow up.

Robert Moorehead

Made in the USA
San Bernardino, CA
21 October 2016